I0804450

21ST CENTURY CHORDS FOR GUITAR

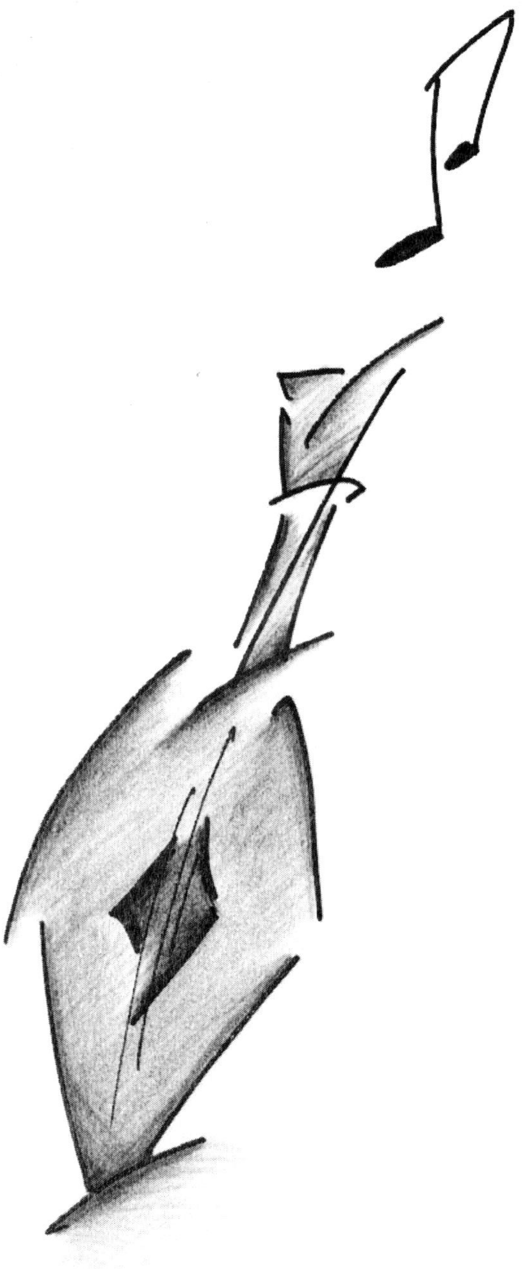

Cover illustration by Katrin Lieske

By Steve Bloom

MEL BAY

CONTENTS

"Anyone looking for a way into non-tonal, non-traditional sounds on the guitar will find a great resource in this well-organized, comprehensive book."...Ben Monder

"This is the most comprehensive chord compilation I have seen to date. Steve has put together an easy to understand text in a creative, useful way!" -- Vic Juris

21st Century Chords for Guitar

Introduction

Hello and welcome to *21st Century Chords for Guitar*! I hope you will find this material fresh, informative and ear opening.

This book presents a new perspective on guitar chords. Most guitarists view chords in a way that I would classify as traditional. The method that most guitarists are taught to practice chords is a standard one which works to "get us through" any accompaniment situation, e.g. gigs and rehearsals. In these pages I have attempted to show that the guitar is much less limited, chordally, than is generally realized.

I have used the theories of 12-tone music, also known as *atonal music*, to generate voicings of all the possible playable "note groups" on the guitar. While I was writing out these chords I learned much more about voicings and the visualization of the fingerboard than I expected. I had no idea it was going to have such a great effect on my own playing. I hope you will have a similar experience by delving into these concepts. My main reason for searching out this information was to improve my own conception of chords on the instrument, and it turned into something I felt would benefit all guitarists.

Most guitar players have a very conventional concept of the voicings they play. I know that a lot of the chords in this book will sound very dissonant compared to what you are used to playing. However, if you dig deeper into the book you will also find interesting voicings for many "everyday" chords that you probably wouldn't figure out using other methods. My goal is to help change the way we as guitar players think of chords on the instrument.

Note Groups

To generate these chords I have used the concept of *Note Groups*. Atonal music theory lists all the possible groups of notes using numbers. For example, C would be 0, C♯ would be 1, D would be 2, etc. until B which is 11 (0 to 11 equals 12 tones). This method allowed me to get away from tonal chord theory and look only at the mathematical relationship between all notes in any group. The note groups have names that are slightly different than in tonal music, and are as follows:

3 notes - Tri-Chords
4 notes - Tetra-Chords
5 notes - Penta-Chords
6 notes - Hexa-Chords

The first Tri-Chord is listed as "012". The zero is pronounced like the letter "O", so this would be the "O-one-two Tri-Chord", consisting of the notes C, C♯ and D. The next Tri-Chord would be 013, consisting of C, C♯ and D♯. The first Tetra-Chord is "0123", consisting of C, C♯, D and D♯. This method of grouping the notes together continues all the way up until the 12-note groups. Obviously, one cannot play 12-note groups on the guitar, so I have stopped at the 6-note groups. At first glance you might think, "Playable chords with 6 separate notes on the guitar? Not too many of those are available!" But if you turn to the section on Hexa-Chords, you will see a lot more of them than might be expected.

One other concept: I have started all of the chords in the book on the note "C". This is to make it easier to relate all the chords to each other. Please realize that any of these chords may be played starting on any of the 12 tones. The reason for thinking in numbers is the same as in tonal music. Any chordal structure will have the same numerical name no matter what note it starts on. For example: Any chord with the same interval structure as "C, C♯, D" will be called an 012 Tri-Chord.

How To Read the Chords

The way the book is set up is very straightforward and I have used the same concept throughout. There are eight sections, one each on Tri-Chords, Tetra-Chords, Penta-Chords, Hexa-Chords and a section for the inversion of each one of those chord types. (See the text below on inversions for more information.) At the beginning of each section, I have put a page showing all of the note groups with their corresponding numbers. On the pages after that, each note group is written out at the start of a new chord, followed by possible voicings. I took each note in the group, put it on the bottom, and attempted to voice a chord on each note in the group. (See Example 1)

Example 1: 012 Tri-Chord:

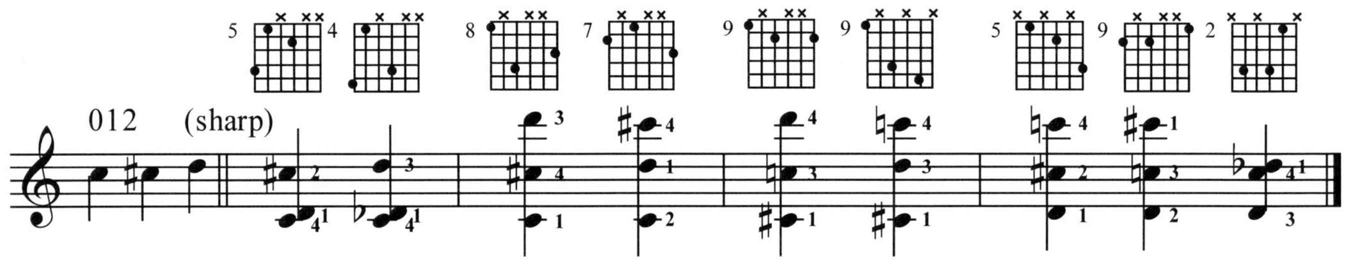

In the first measure the notes of the chord are written as a short line. All of the chords are written this way so that it is easier to visualize which notes are in a given chord. In this example there is a chord built on each of the notes C, C♯, and D. The number of the chord (012) is written above those first notes and sometimes you will see a description of the sound (i.e. "sharp", "bland", etc.) or an actual tonal chord name. This is to help bridge the gap between tonal and atonal perspectives.

The chords are written out in standard notation, a guitar chord frame above each one, and fret-hand fingering numbers next to the notes. The fret number of the chord frames is to the left of each frame, and the fingering numbers are to the right of the notes.

In some cases there wasn't a playable voicing on every note, and sometimes there wasn't a playable voicing at all. Even if there wasn't a voicing for a given chord, I have included it anyway. There is always the possibility that there is a voicing starting from a note other than "C". I didn't put transpositions in the book because it would become too confusing if I started doing that in addition to all the other concepts. If you find voicings for these chords, then you will really get what these concepts are all about. The only two sections that have note groups with "unplayable" voicings are the Hexa-Chords and Inverted Hexa-Chords.

Techniques & Theory

a) Fingerings

I have included many challenging fingerings as well as easier voicings. All the chords *are* playable (I have played them myself). Some chords may be more suited for people with longer fingers, or a shorter scale guitar, etc. For the record, I have average-length fingers.

Sometimes you may need to do things like reach around with the thumb, play two strings with the tip of one finger, or slant the first finger across two frets. Also, some of the chords are easier to play if you use the right-hand fingers or a pick-and-fingers approach because of unusual string groupings. Many of the chords are technically very easy and you will be surprised that you don't need a lot of technique to play these sounds, unusual or familiar.

Please note: these are *not* the only fingerings. Many of the chords have alternate fingerings, especially the 3- and 4-note groups. I use four fingers more often than barring because it is easier to voice lead between chords. If you prefer to barre the chords, or use any other fingering method, feel free to do so. Many guitarists might prefer to play the chords in different positions, use other string groupings, etc. Play through the written fingerings, as there are many interesting ideas embedded in the chords over the course of the book. Take any of the ideas here and find the best way to make them your own. Experiment!

b) Rotation

The atonal word for inversion is *rotation*. The word inversion, in tonal music, means playing a chord with each successive note as the lowest tone. This generates more than one form of each chord. *Rotation* has the same function in that you take the lowest note in a chord and move it above the other notes in the chord or "note group". I have voiced out every *rotation* for each chord in the book. (See Ex. 2)

c) Tonal vs. Atonal Chord Naming

Since I covered all possible note groups, many of the chords are tonal in nature. Each chord is labeled with the atonal number – 0158, etc, and the tonal name, if possible, as in Ex. 2 below – "D♭maj7".

When a chord is tonal, I arranged the chords in guitar inversions going up the neck. (See Ex. 2) The concept is to take the notes of the arpeggio and move each note to the next one on the SAME STRING. Thinking up and down each string is the quickest way to learn the instrument. Sitar players, for example, have been thinking that way for centuries. If you think this way, you will get faster results, and find chords you wouldn't find otherwise.

Example 2: 0158 Tetra-Chord, or D♭Maj7:
(Excerpt, see Tetra-Chord section for the rest.)

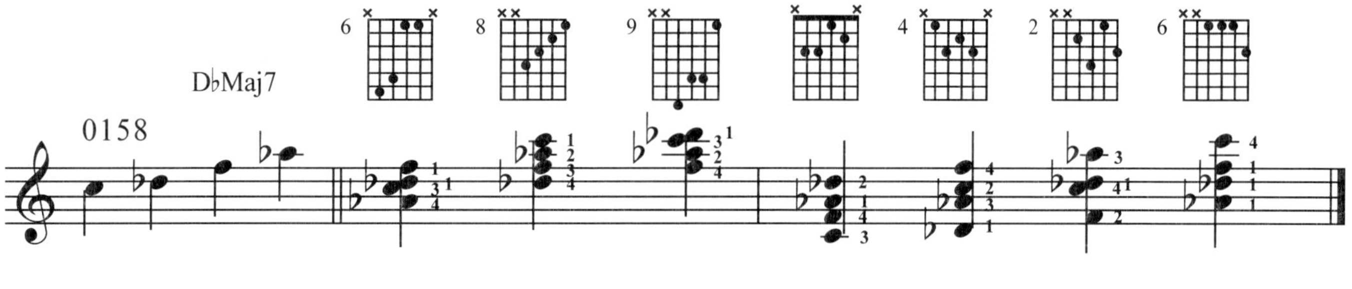

d) Voicings: Open vs. Fretted Strings

Wherever possible I have avoided using open strings so that the chords may be transposed anywhere up and down the neck. However, many of the chords can *only* be played using open strings. This is especially true in the sections on the 5 and 6-note groups.

Feel free to come up with new voicings for these chords; I'm sure I haven't found them all. Also, try them on different frets. If a chord is too difficult lower down, try it higher up where the frets are closer together. Also, you can move them down so that some of the strings are open. Some of them also sound interesting on different types of guitars, or with effects, different pickup choices, with a volume pedal, etc.

One voicing idea that happens very often is that a chord might be played higher up the neck but there are open strings in the chord. In order to make many of the chords playable I had to use every string combination. So it is possible that a chord could be played in 10th position, for example, but you might have one or two open strings at the same time. The fret number is indicated to the left of each chord frame but watch out for the open-string notations.

Inversions

Inversion in atonal music doesn't mean the same thing as in tonal music. In a tonal chord, the bottom note is moved one octave higher, or the top note is moved one octave lower. In atonal theory this is called a *rotation*, as explained previously. All the chords in this book are generated using the idea of *rotation*. The atonal perspective on *inversion* is to view the intervals of the chord as in a mirror image. For example, if you had a chord of only two notes, C and D, the *inversion* of that interval would be C *down* to B♭. In the first chord there is an ascending whole step interval and in the second chord, a descending whole step interval. Look at the next example that shows the *inversion* of a Tri-Chord.

Example 3: Inversion of an 037 Tri-Chord or C minor triad:

From the note C, the C minor triad goes up a minor third to E♭ and then, from E♭, up a major third to G. The *inversion*, starting from C, goes down a minor third to A and then, from A, down a major third to F. Structurally these two chords are mirror images of each other. Therefore, according to atonal music theory, these two chords are *inversions* of each other.

There are two types of *inversions* in atonal music: *non-symmetrical* and *symmetrical*. A *non-symmetrical* inversion is shown in Example 3 above, where the two chords are not exactly the same. Most of the inversions in the book are of this type. The other type, *symmetrical* inversion, is slightly different. When you are finished inverting the second chord, it will be exactly the same structure intervallically as the original.

Example 4: Symmetrical inversion of an 036 Tri-Chord or C diminished triad:

Take a look at Ex. 4. In the first measure, C goes up a min 3rd to E♭, which goes up a min 3rd to G♭. In the second measure C goes down a min 3rd to A, which goes down a min 3rd to F♯. According to atonal theory, these two chords are the *same thing* because they are intervalically, or structurally, exact mirror images of each other.

When you start playing through the inverted sections of each note group (i.e., Inverted Tri-Chords, etc.), the symmetrical chords will be listed as such. These chords generally won't be written out again, since they are structurally the same. However, there are some exceptions because I found some interesting shapes or the combination of open and fretted strings makes the same structures visually unrecognizable on the fingerboard. All of the symmetrical note groups are labeled as such in the inverted sections.

How to Practice

1. The first and most immediately productive method of practicing these voicings is as follows: Flip through the book until you find a tonal chord name that you are familiar with. Play through the voicings of only that chord for a few days, a week, or even longer. After that you will be used to the chord and you should be able to use it in a live playing situation or for composing, etc. Since the book is a reference, you can use it over a long period of time. When you find a tonal group that has inversions up and down the guitar fretboard, practice switching between the voicings until you can play them smoothly.

2. Take one chord and follow it through its evolution in each section. For example, take the 014 Tri-Chord. When you get to the Tetra-Chord section, you will see that there are 4 Tetra-Chords built on the 014 Tri-Chord. If you know the Tri-Chord very well, it will be easier to visualize the Tetra-Chord. This concept continues into the other sections as well.

3. Other ways of using these chords in tonal situations will come up as you dig into the material. For example, any note-group using whole steps will generally work over Dom7(♭5) or (♯5) chords.

4. Another way to work with this material is to look at it from an atonal perspective. The nice thing, to me, about calling these chords by their number name as opposed to "C7" etc., is that it changes your thinking process. The chords become SOUNDS. They create a different energy when viewed in this manner. If you can get away from the traditional idea of the function of a chord, you will open up a new world of sounds to yourself and your audience.

Using All 12 Notes

Since it is not possible, as on a piano, to play a chord of all 12 notes at once, you can cycle through all 12 notes using various chord combinations. Groups of two Hexa-Chords, three Tetra-Chords, or four Tri-

Chords, as well as any other combination, will all work. In order to set this up properly, you must arrange what is called a *tone row* in advance.

A tone row, is a "scale" using all 12 notes. The most obvious tone row is the chromatic scale. Let's break up the chromatic scale into component parts as an exercise. The chromatic scale could be broken up into the following groups:

Four 012 Tri-Chords
Three 0123 Tetra-Chords
Two 012345 Hexa-Chords

Example 5:

Line 1 has a Tri-Chord built on C, D♯, F♯, and A,
Line 2 has a Tetra-Chord built on C, E, and G♯,
Line 3 has a Hexa-Chord built on C and F♯.

The name for each note group is written above each measure. You will find voicings for each of these note groups in the appropriate section in the book. For example, go to the Tetra-Chords section, look up the 0123 chords and transpose voicings to each of the above notes, and you have a substantial set of chord groups.

The concept here is that you take each note group and build a chord using only those notes. In the case of Ex. 4 all the chords will sound the same because the starting row is the chromatic scale. I chose the chromatic scale as a beginning point. Of course, it is possible to arrange a tone row by choosing any group of notes. Instead of using only one Tri-Chord, it is possible to arrange a tone row using various groups of notes within one row. Let's see what happens if we build some chords using different Tri-, Tetra-, and Hexa- Chords.

The row I now choose is as follows:

A C♯ B♭ B G♯ F♯ D D♯ E F G C

I did not start this row from C. I started all the chords in the book on C but, of course, all chords and tone rows may be transposed to any note. Look at Example 6 below to see this row written out with labeled note groups.

Example 6:

This row is a lot more interesting than the one in Example 5. There are a lot of ideas happening here. Why did I choose this particular arrangement of notes? In atonal music, you will find that choices are made based on what type of sound area the composer wishes to create. I happen to like the 012 Tri-Chord a lot, so I wanted to include at least one. I also wanted to have a "suspended" or "fourths" sound so I included an 027 Tri-Chord, which has that character. This left me with six notes so I analyzed what was left.

Over time, you will become used to the sound of each chord or group, just as in tonal music you can hear the difference between a major and a minor chord. An 012 Tri-Chord has a very different character than an 027 or an 014, or any other group.

I began this row thinking about four different Tri-Chords. The Tetra- and Hexa-Chords that I found after that were not planned. For example, I was not expecting to arrive at two of the same Hexa-Chords; that was a surprise. The Tetra-Chords are also very nice. By the way, you could also arrange your row as one Penta-Chord, one Tri-Chord, and one Tetra-Chord; the possibilities are up to you.

Once you have come up with your row and analyzed the chords, you have many voicing choices. You could simply find voicings based on the notes in the row, or you could look up your chord choices in the book and get ideas that way.

Normal Form

Another question raises itself at this point: How does one figure out which number/name goes with a group of notes?

In atonal theory, there is a concept called the *normal form*. In tonal music, the equivalent concept for the words *normal form* is Root Position. If you have the notes G, C, and E in tonal music, it is common knowledge that this is a C major triad, and that C, E, G would be the root position of that chord. Atonal chords or note groups have an equivalent process in order to figure out the original name for the group. In order to find the *normal form* you check all rotations and find the one with the smallest distance between the root (0) and the outer interval.

In atonal music, intervals are listed by counting half-steps. C to E would be 0-4. The distance from the note C to the note E is 4 half-steps. The largest interval in atonal will be 11. Intervals larger than 11 are then figured from 0 again: 12 would be 0, 13 would be 1, 14 would be 2, etc. In other words, base 12 mathematics.

Let's take the notes E, C♯, and C. In relation to "C", C=0, C♯=1, and E=4. If we list all three rotations, we obtain three different numbers for the outer interval:

1. C C♯ E = 0,1,4 = 4 half-steps
2. C♯ E C = 1,0,4 = 11 half-steps
3. E C C♯ = 4,1,0 = 9 half-steps

The smallest outer interval is rotation 1, therefore 014 is the normal form of C C♯ and E and is the name of that Tri-Chord. You can repeat this process with any note group. However, it gets a lot more complicated when you have a Tetra-, Penta-, or Hexa-Chord. Very often I will check my answers with a published list of all note groups.

Conclusion

I hope you will enjoy the material in this volume. There is a lot of information here, and there is plenty of room for development. In the preceding text I have tried to give an overview of some 12-tone techniques. There is a lot more theory than is explained here, however; I explained only what I thought would be relevant to chord formation. One thing about 12-tone theory, there is a lot of math involved, i.e. formulas, theorems, equations, etc. I did not get into that for the sake of brevity and clearness. An excellent book, if you are looking for more information is *The Structure of Atonal Music* by Allen Forte, 1973, Yale University Press. I'm sure there are many other texts as well.

Please take this material and run with it! As guitarists, the way we play chord voicings gives us a unique sound. You can change the entire sound and energy of any group you are in, just by the type of chords you choose. It is possible to always find new ways to play chords and I hope this book will be a springboard in that direction. I feel that these ideas will help you in the search to find your own voice. I hope you will enjoy looking through these pages as much as I enjoyed writing them down.

I would like to thank the following people for all the help and advice I have received over the years: I couldn't have done any of this without you!

Henry Martin, Reggie Workman, Maya Milenović, Vic Juris, Pat Martino, Andrea Lieske (my love) for all the wonderful text editing, Adam Rafferty, Ron Gonzalez, Danny Gonzalez, Martin Mueller, and anyone else who listened to me while getting through this book.

Steve Bloom
New York City, Summer 2003

Tri-Chords

012
013
014
(min/maj)
015
(Maj7)
016
024
(Maj9)
025
(min7)
026
(dom7)
027
036
(dim)
037
(minor)
048
(aug)

Tri-Chords

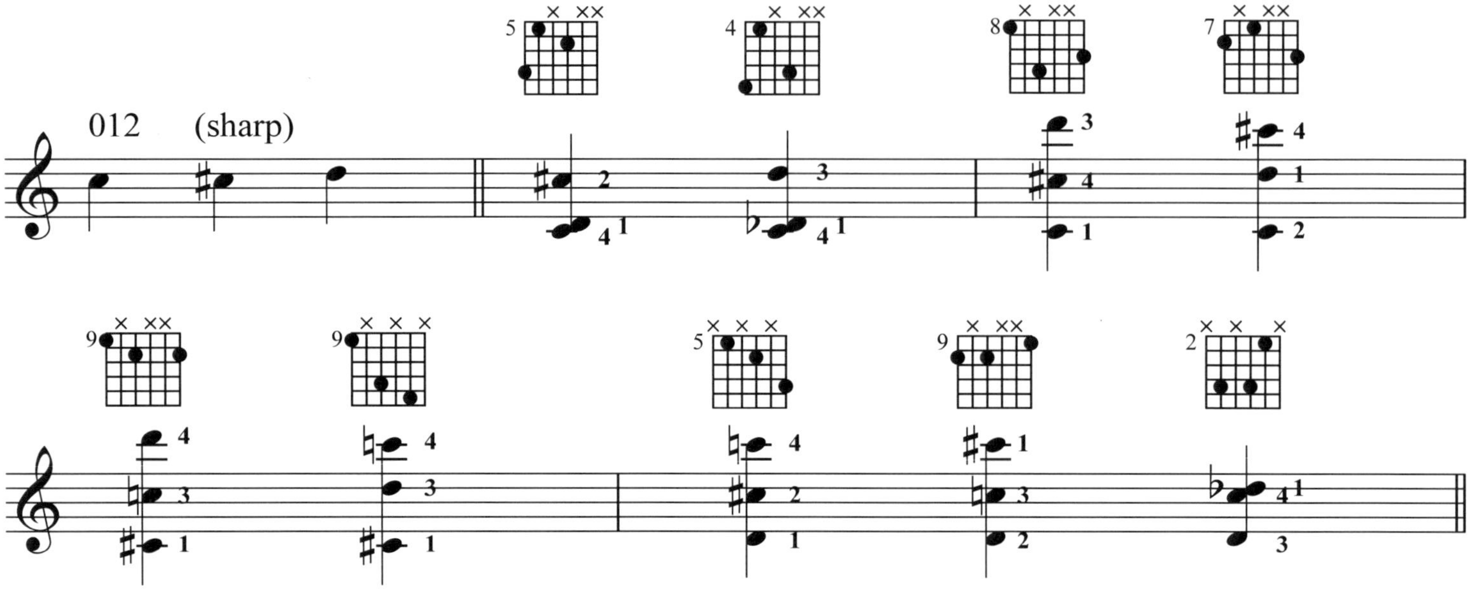

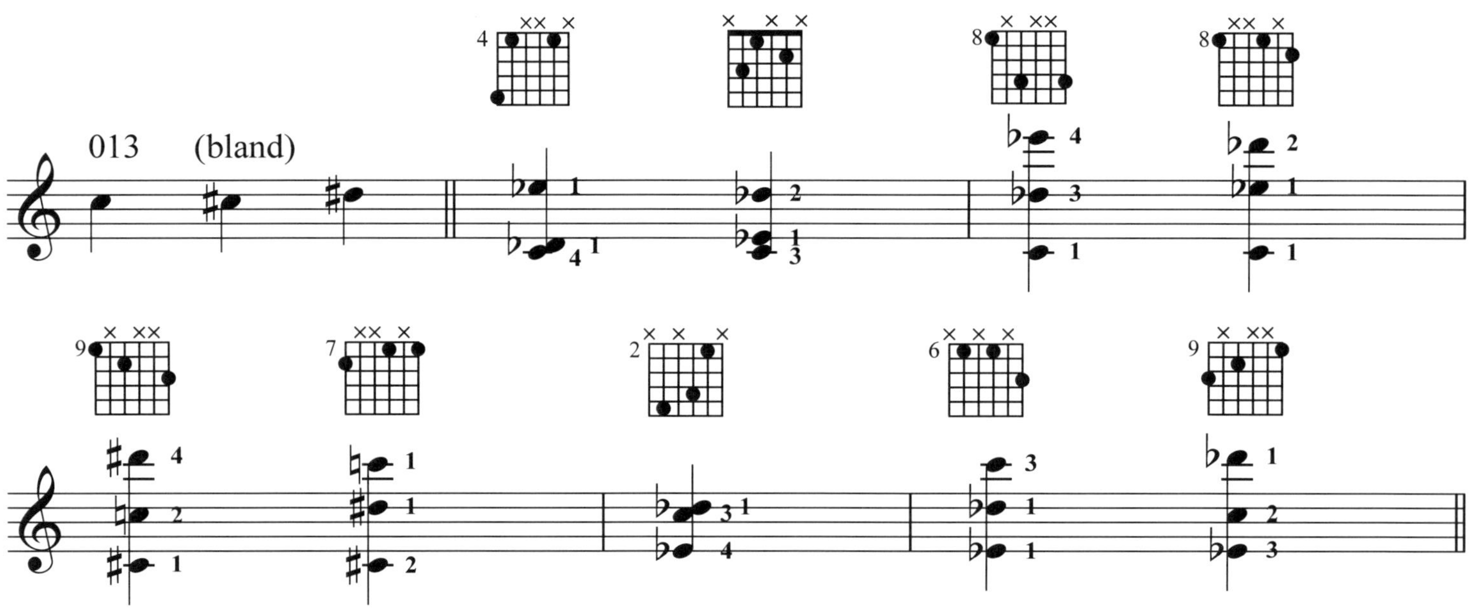

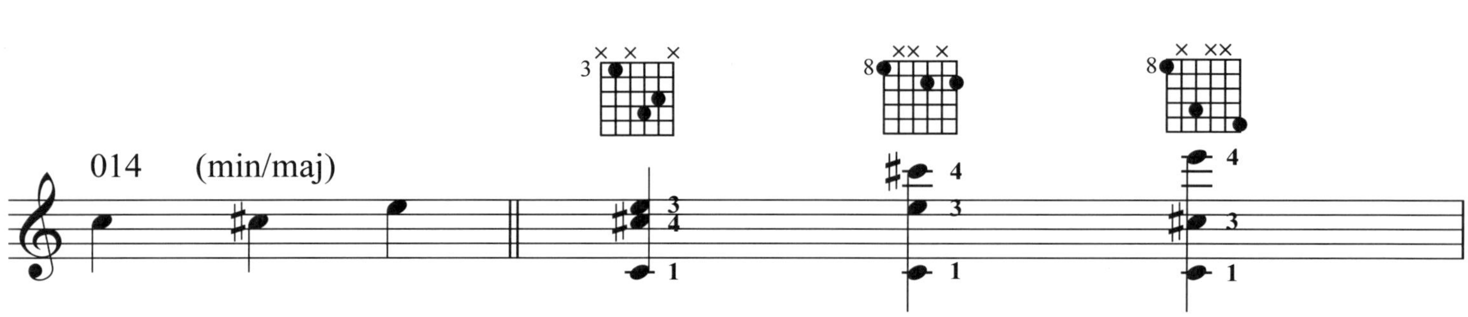

014

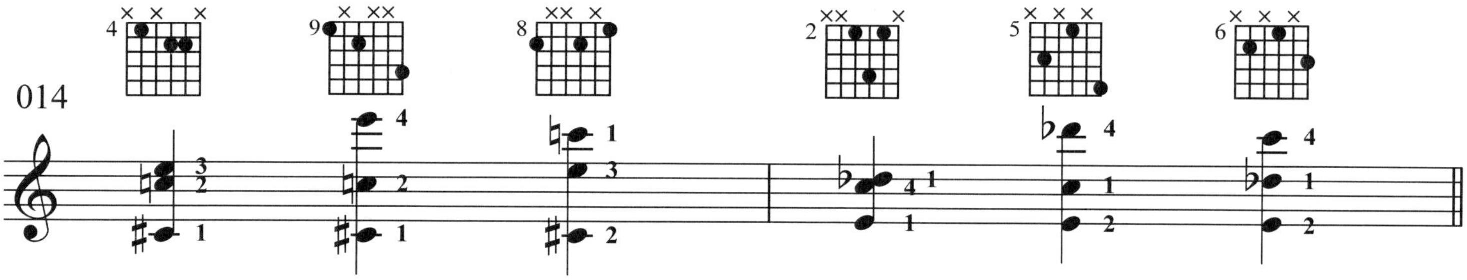

015 (Maj7)

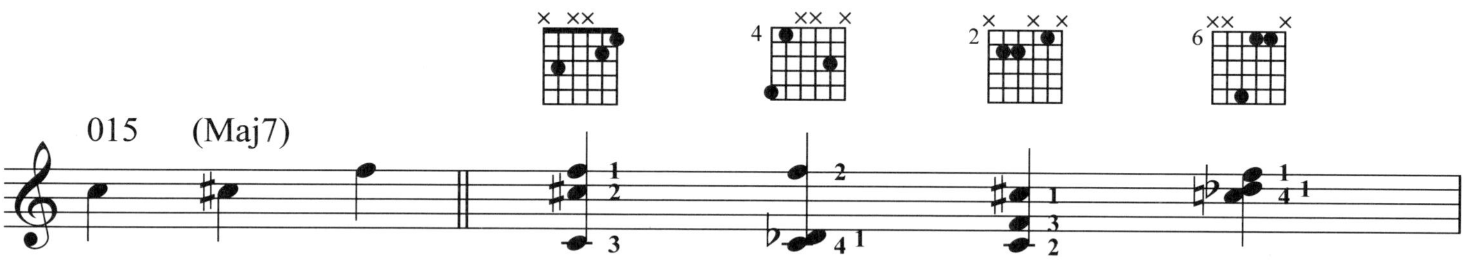

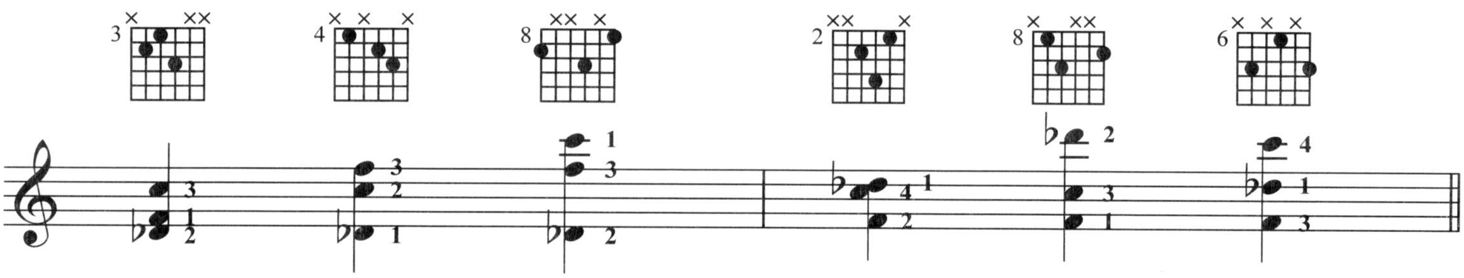

016 (sharp)

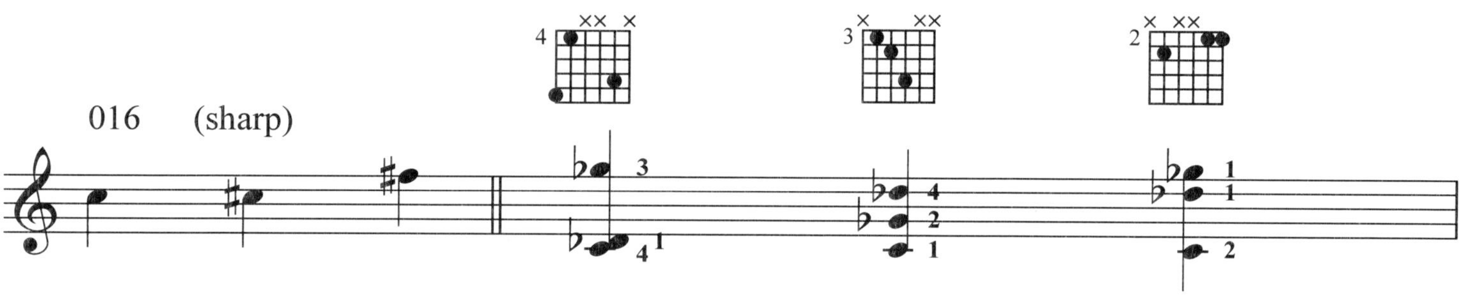

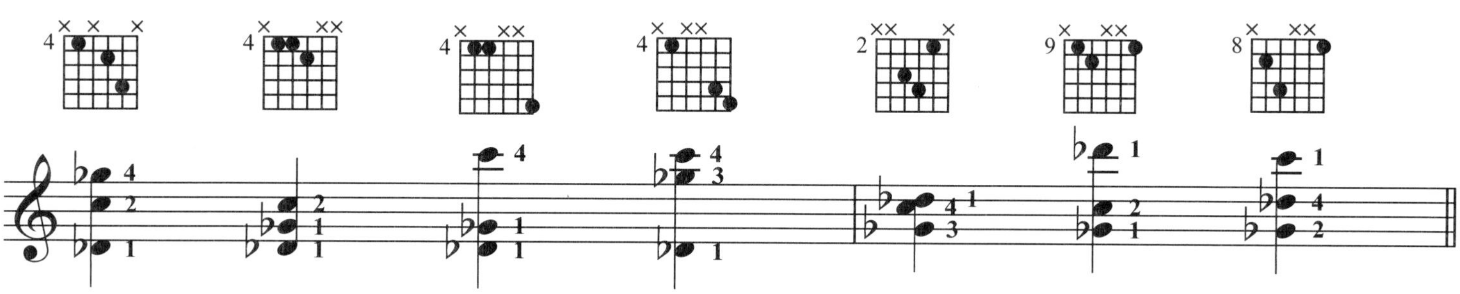

024 (Maj9)

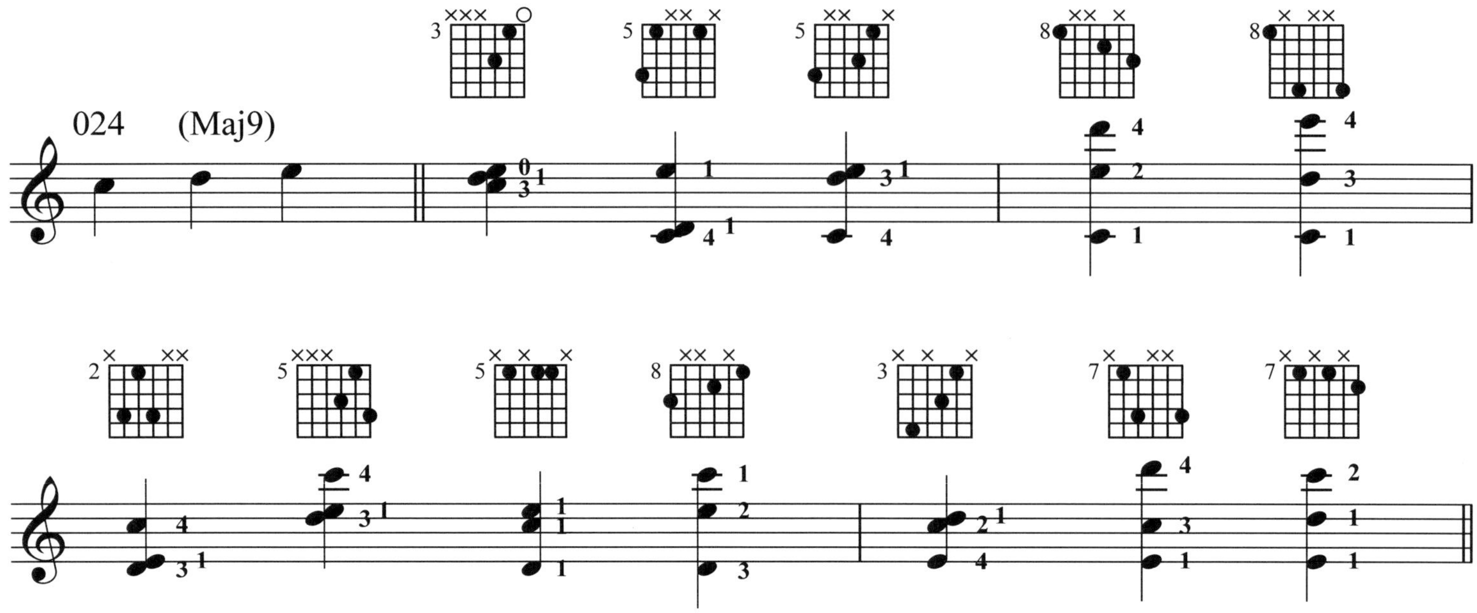

025 (min7)

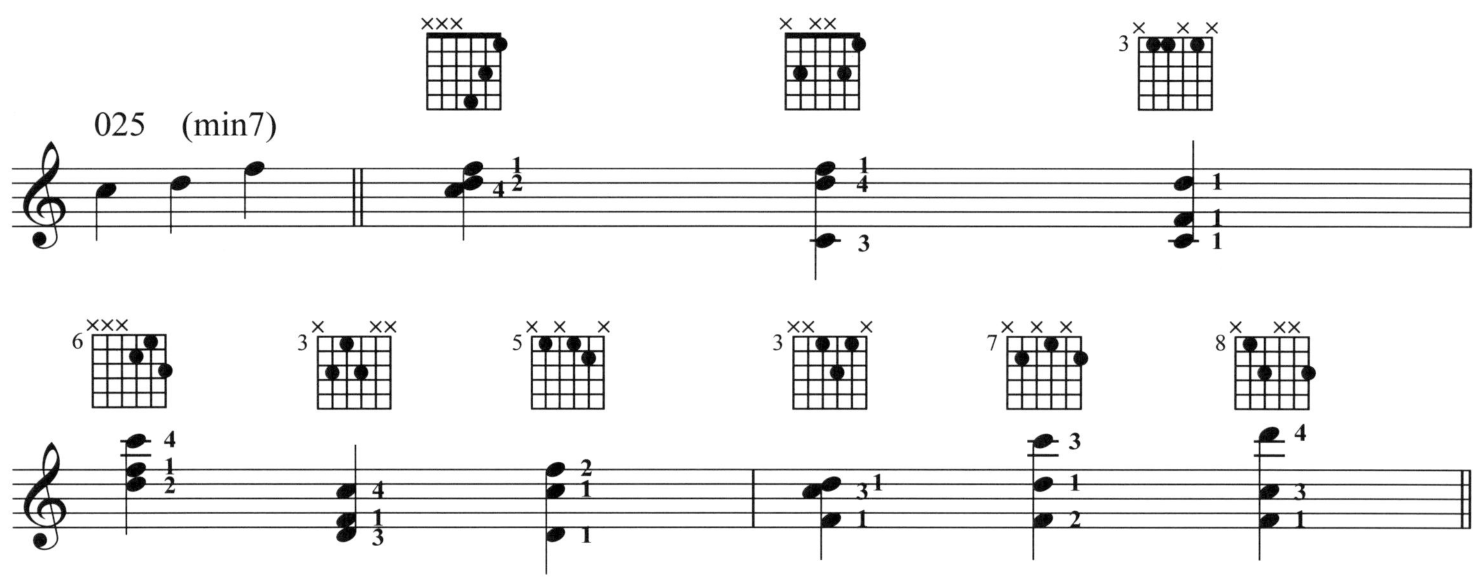

026 (dom7)

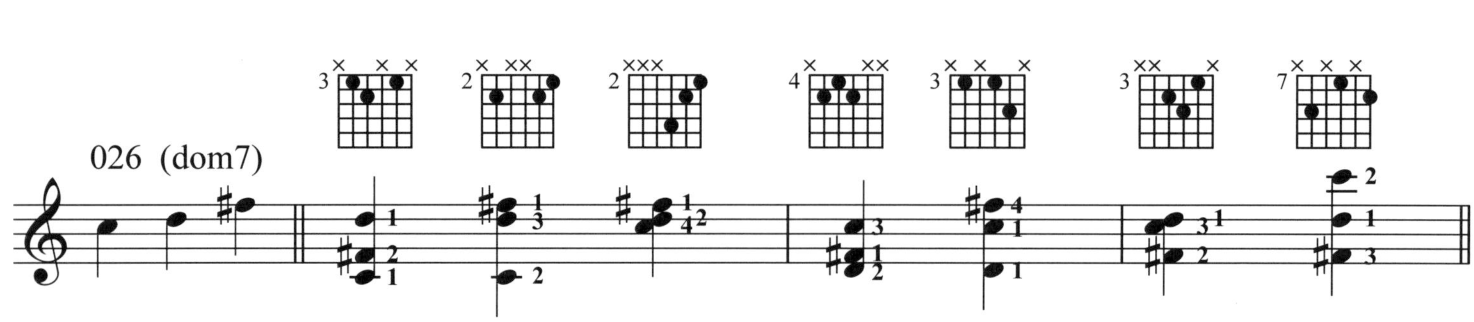

027 ("McCoy")

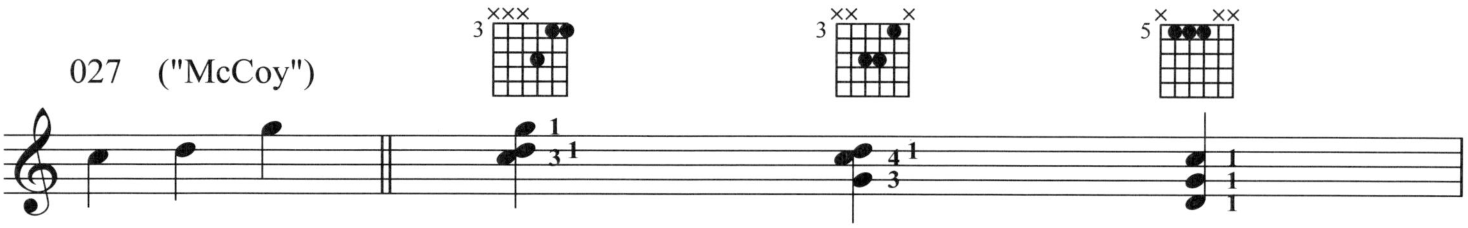

027

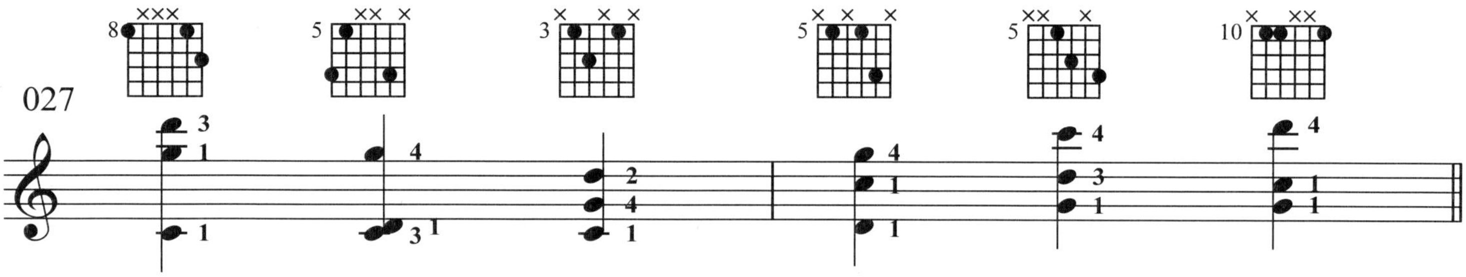

036 (diminished)

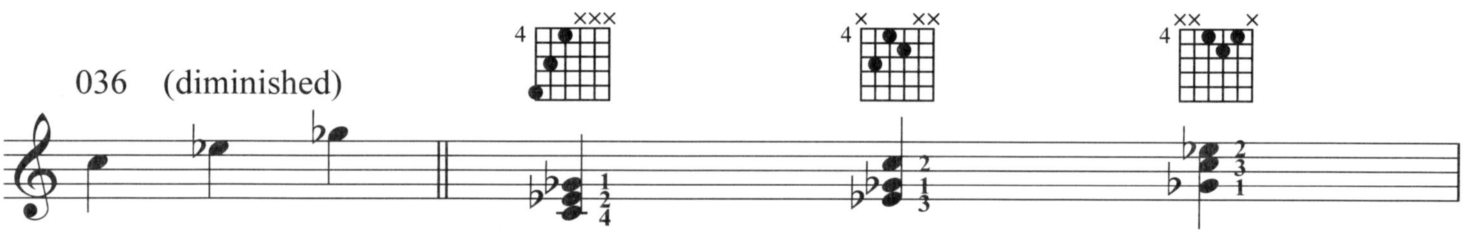

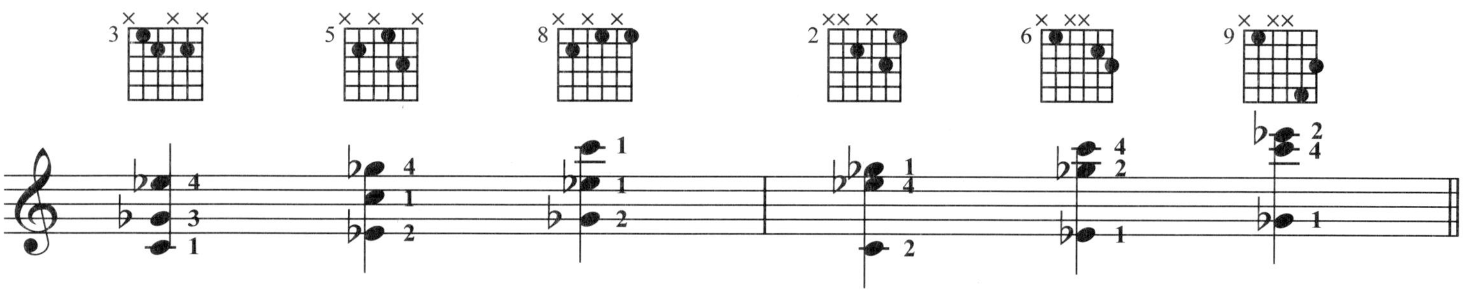

037 (min)

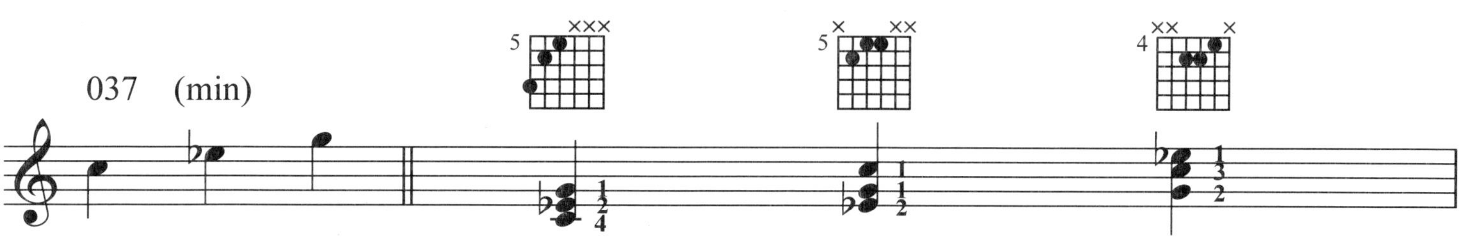

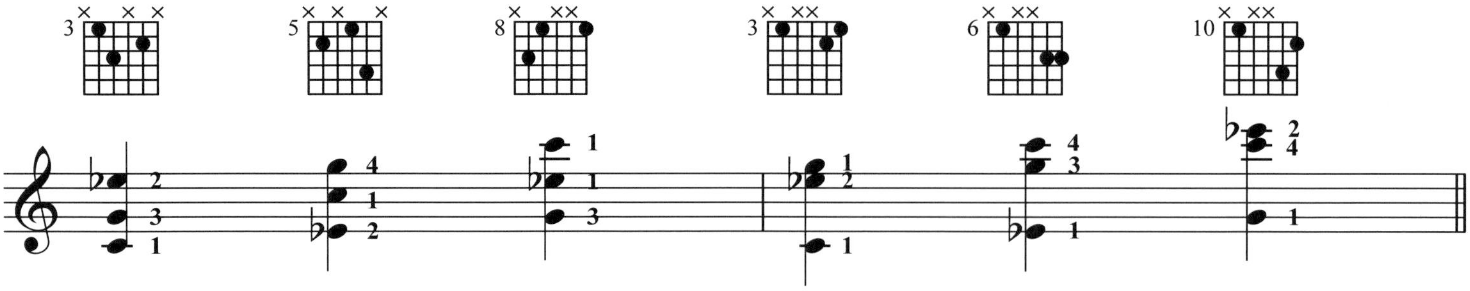

048 (aug)

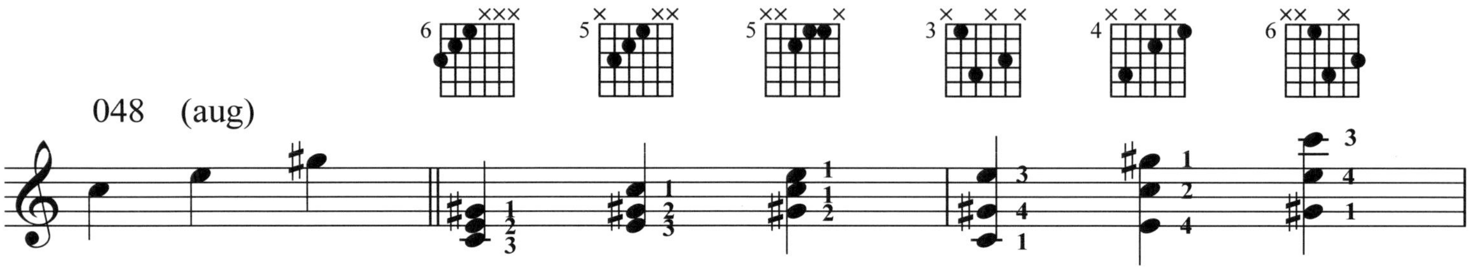

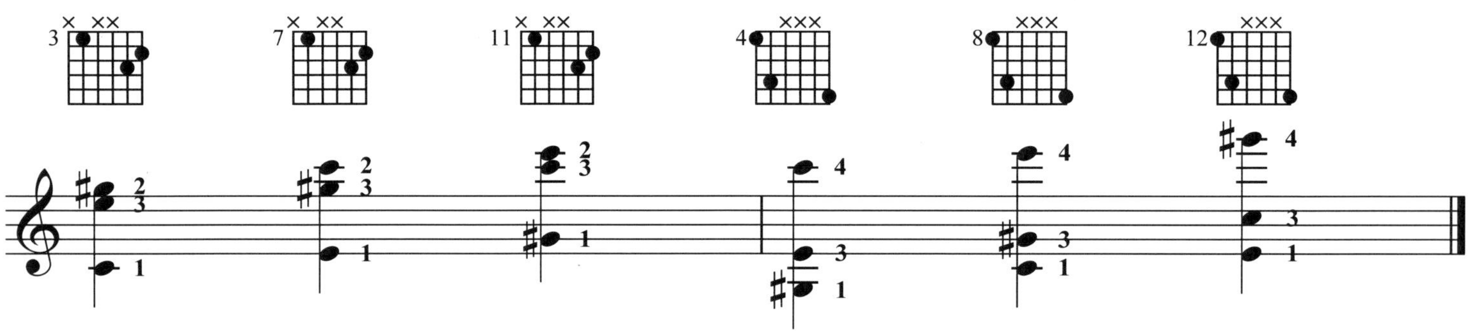

Inverted Tri-Chords

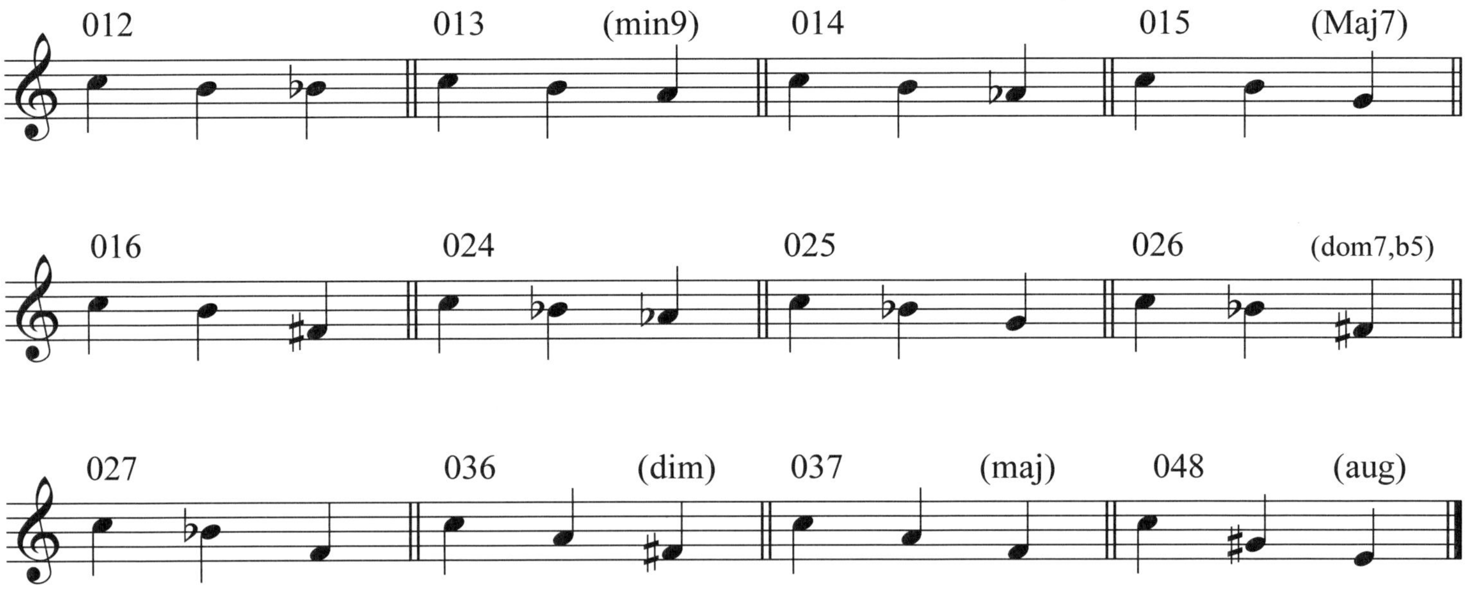

Inverted Tri-Chords

012 Symmetrical (same as 012, previous section)

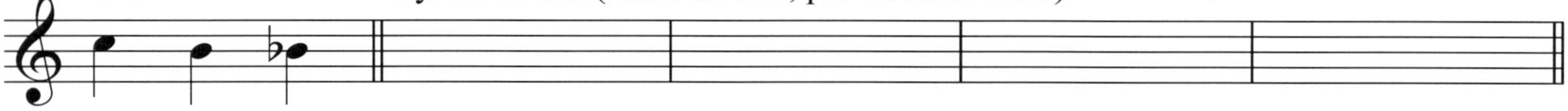

013 (min9)

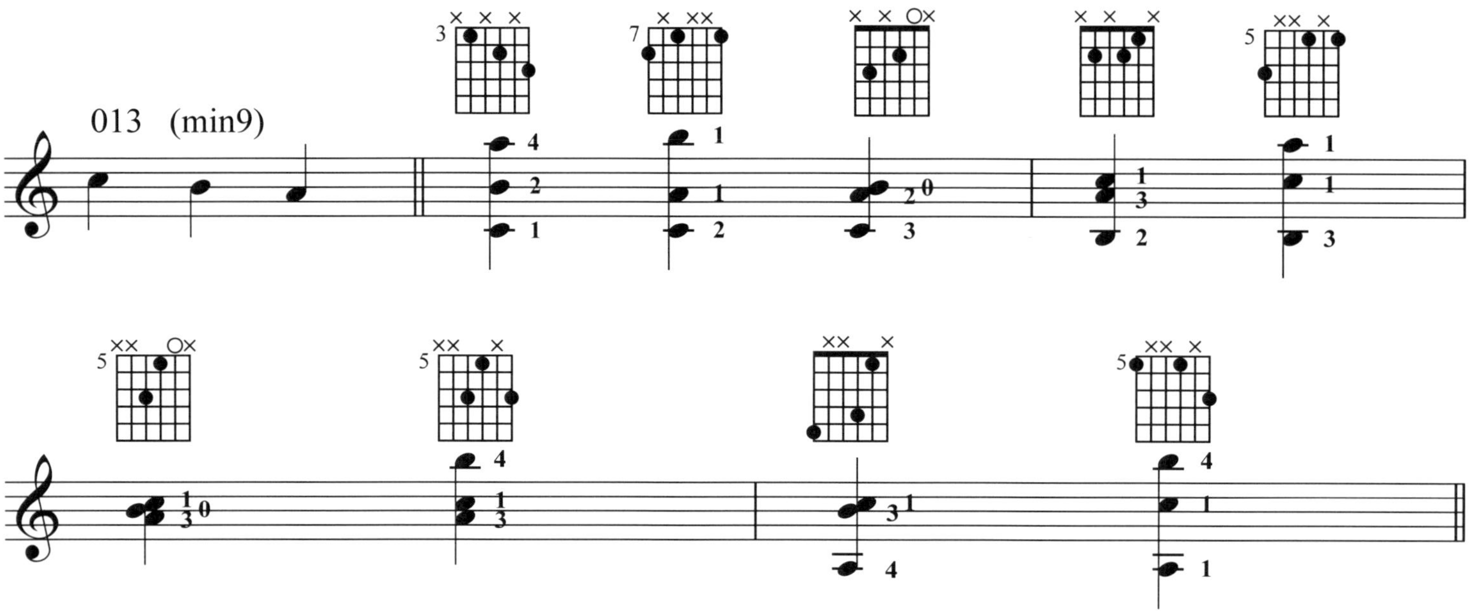

014

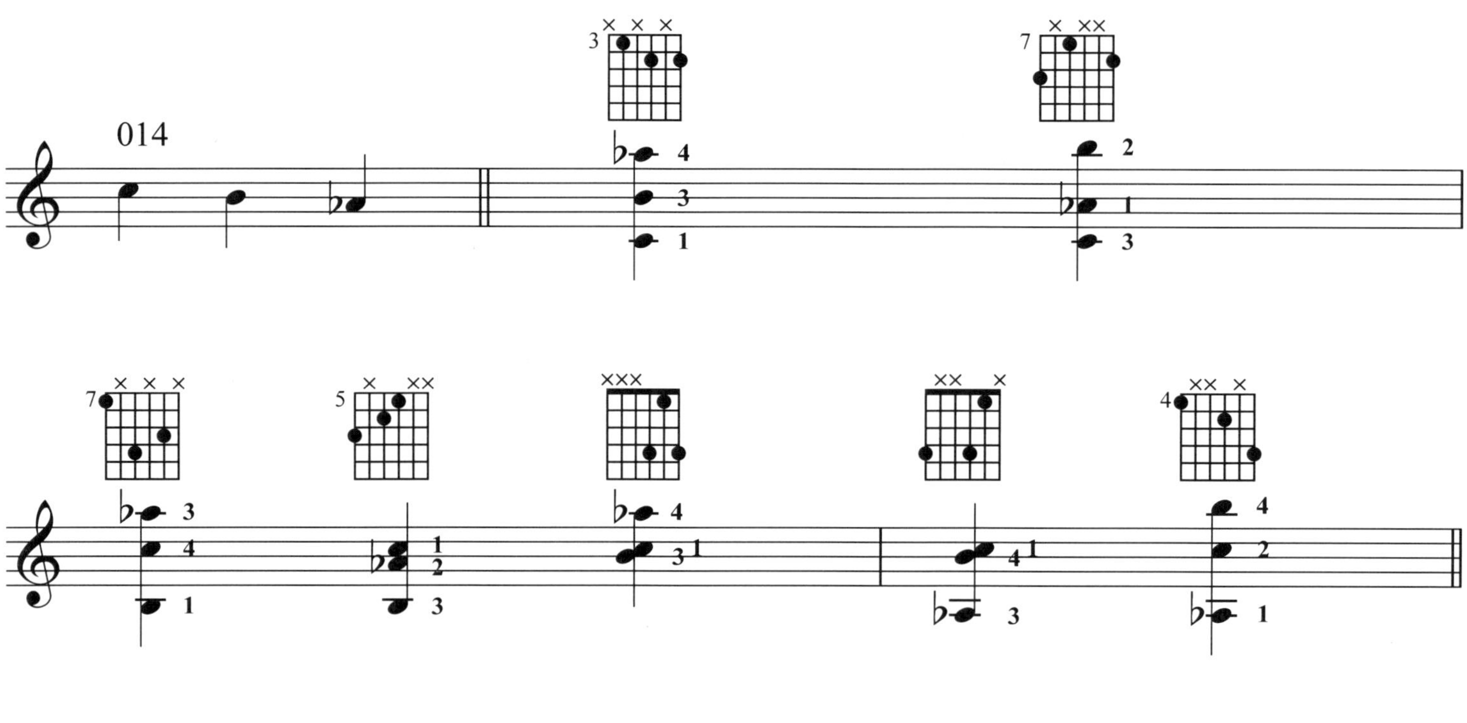

015 (Maj7)

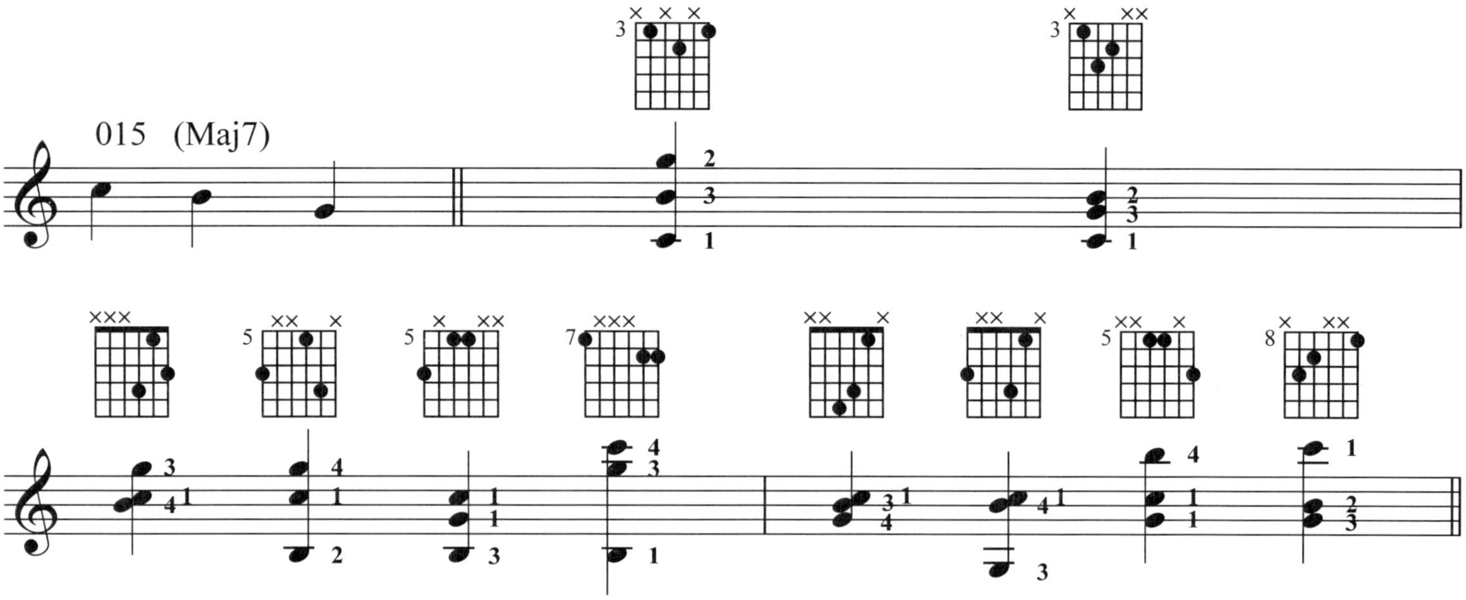

016

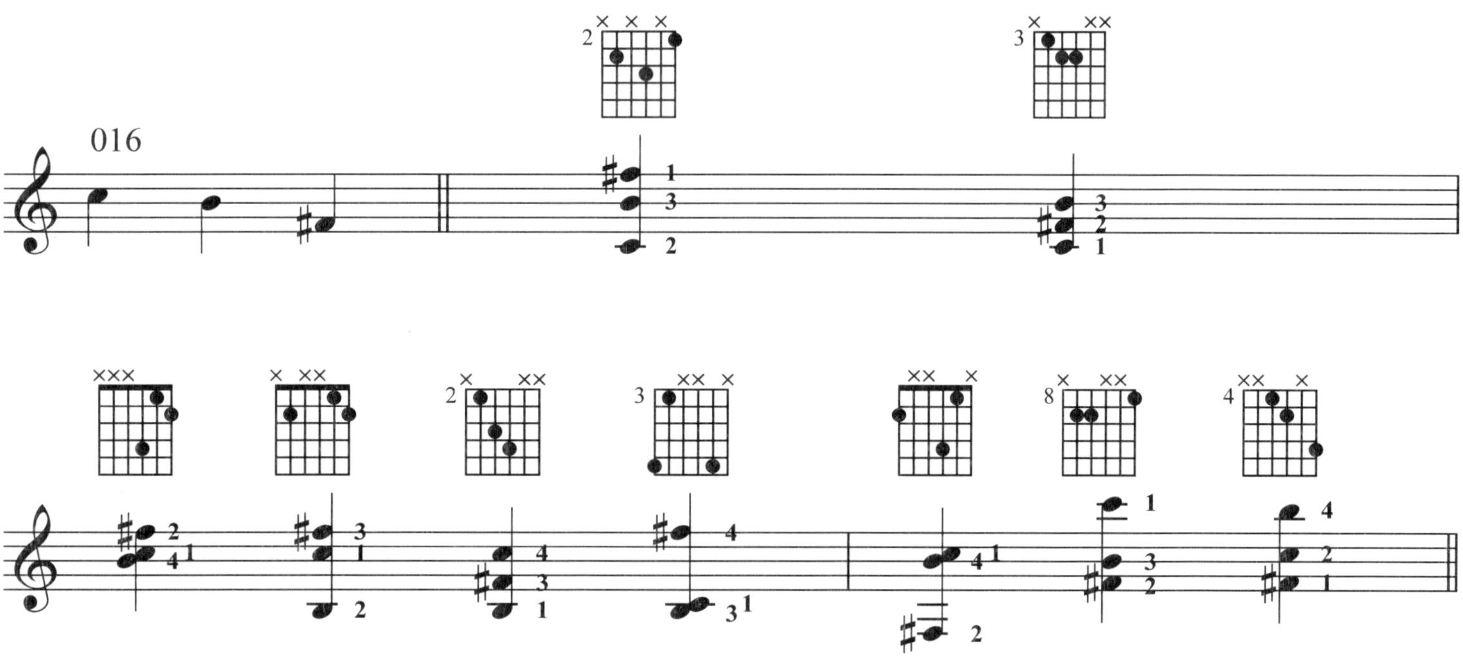

024

Symmetrical (same as 024, previous section)

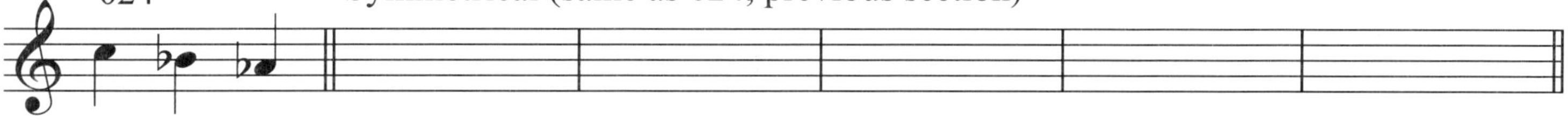

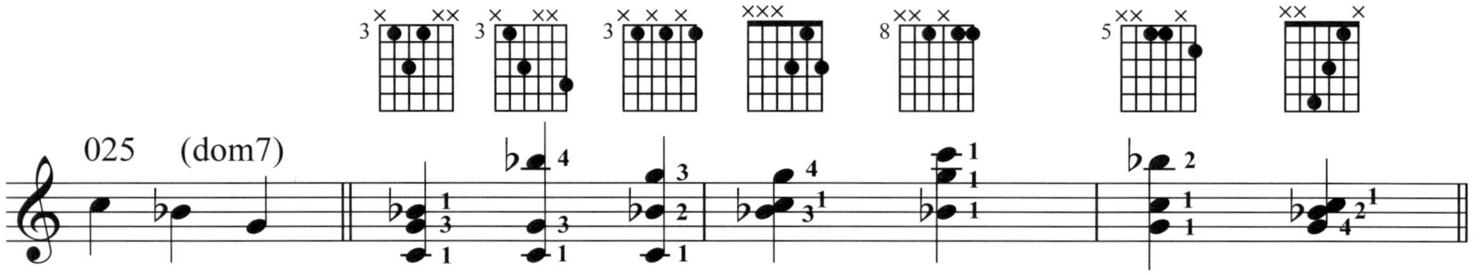
025 (dom7)

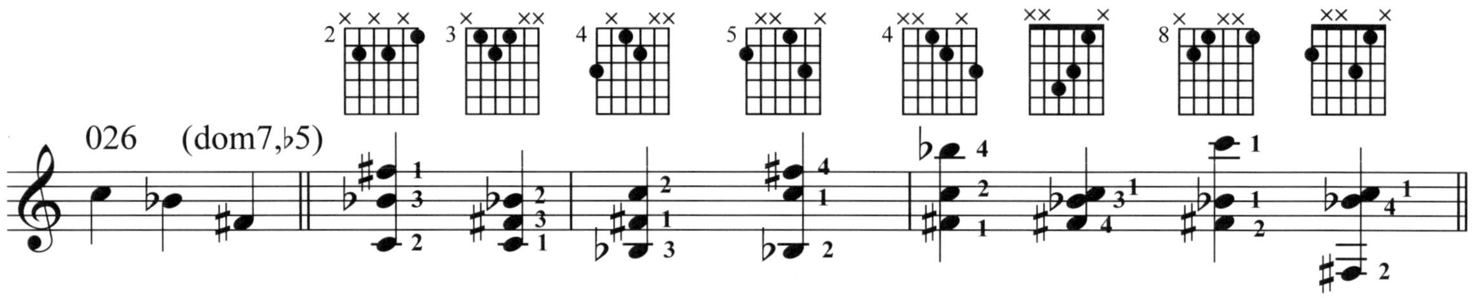
026 (dom7,♭5)

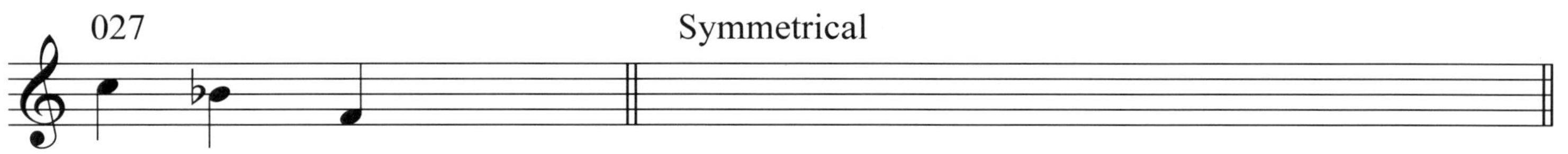
027
Symmetrical

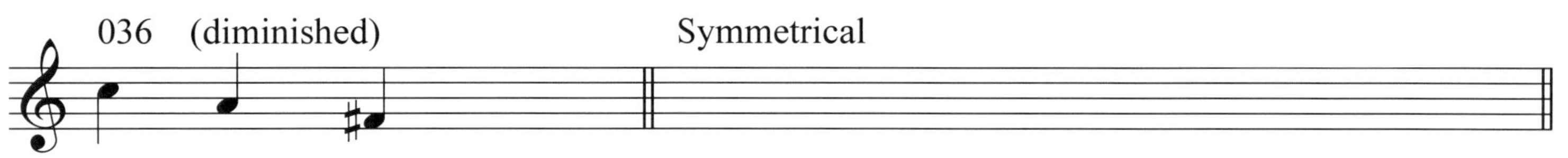
036 (diminished)
Symmetrical

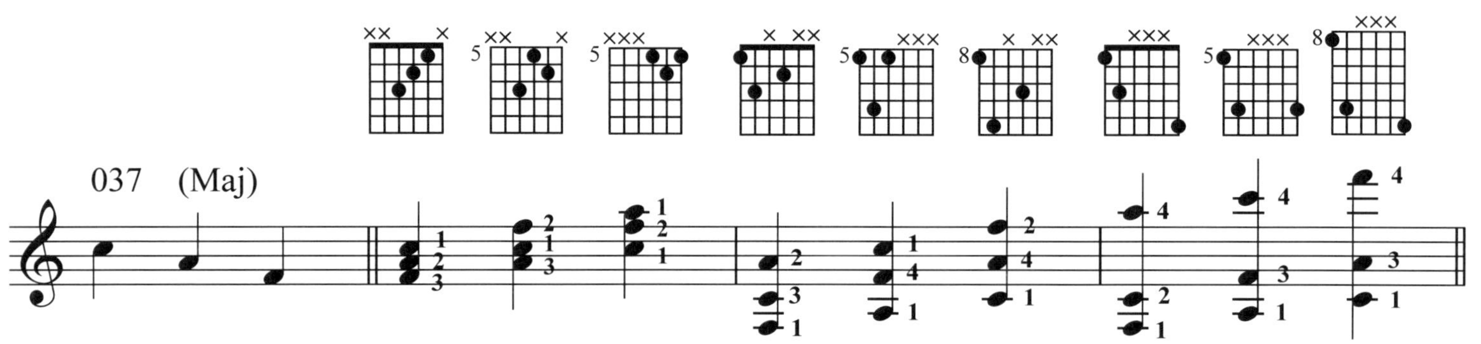
037 (Maj)

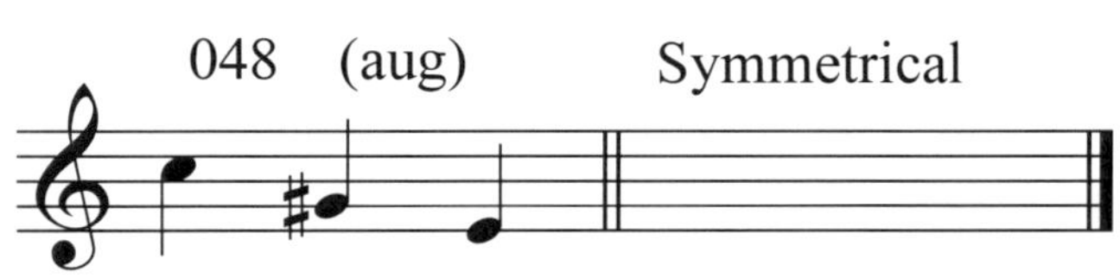
048 (aug)
Symmetrical

Tetra-Chords

Tetra-Chords

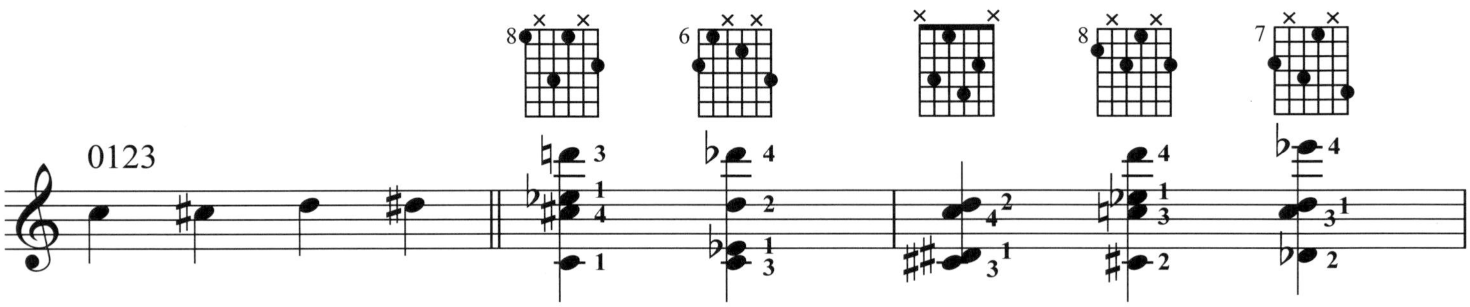

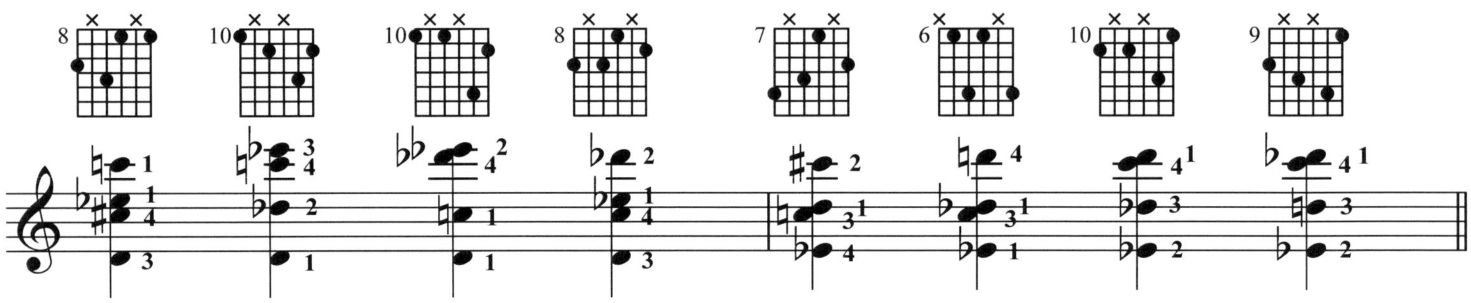

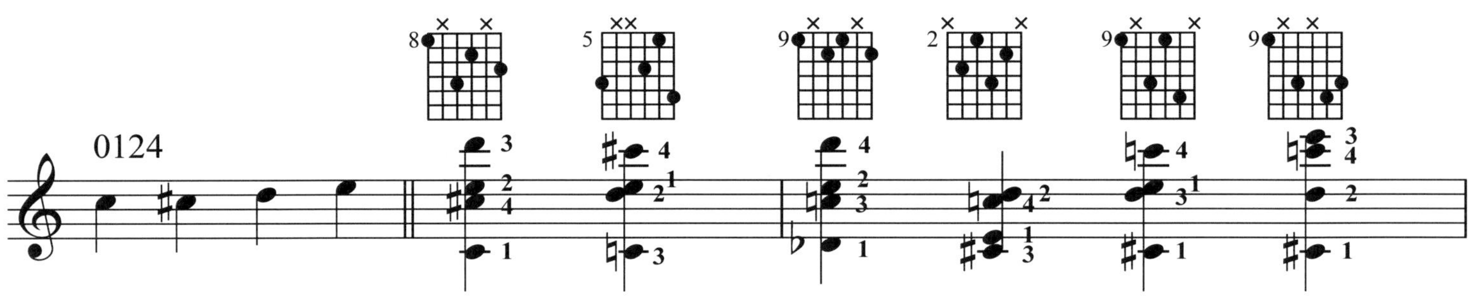

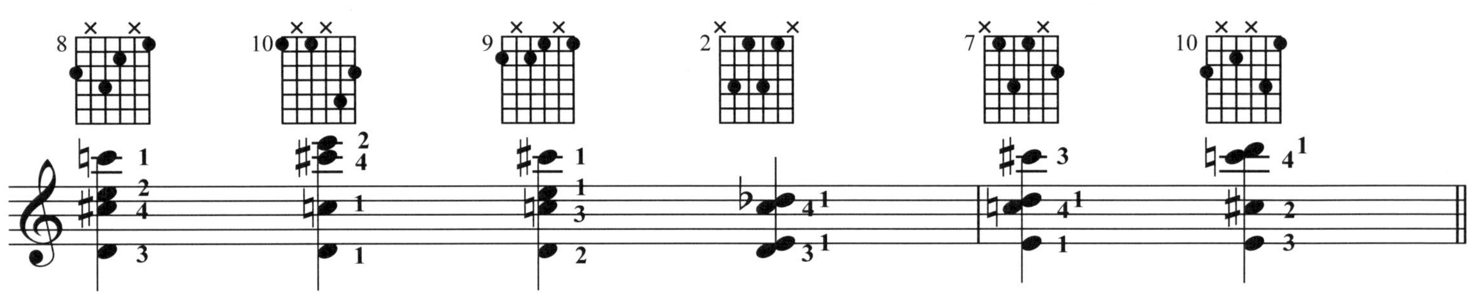

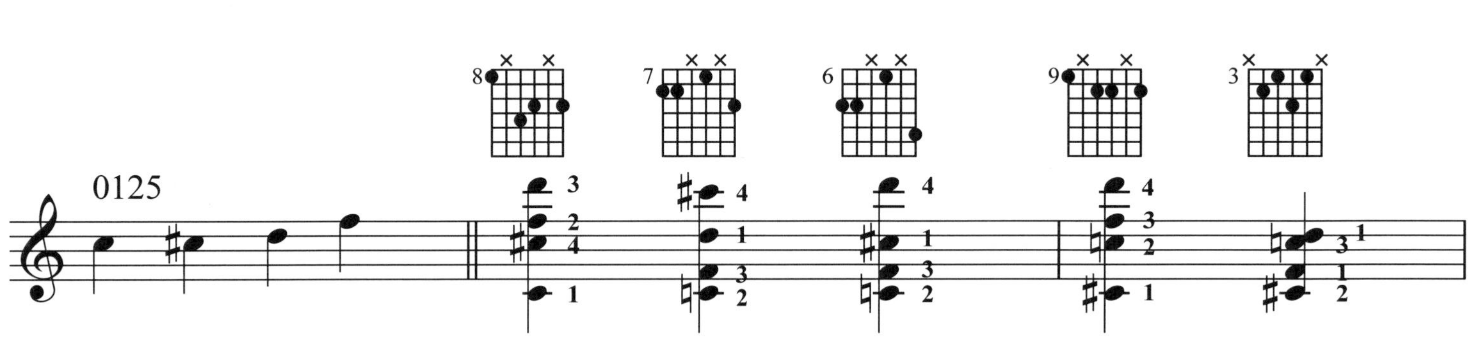

0125

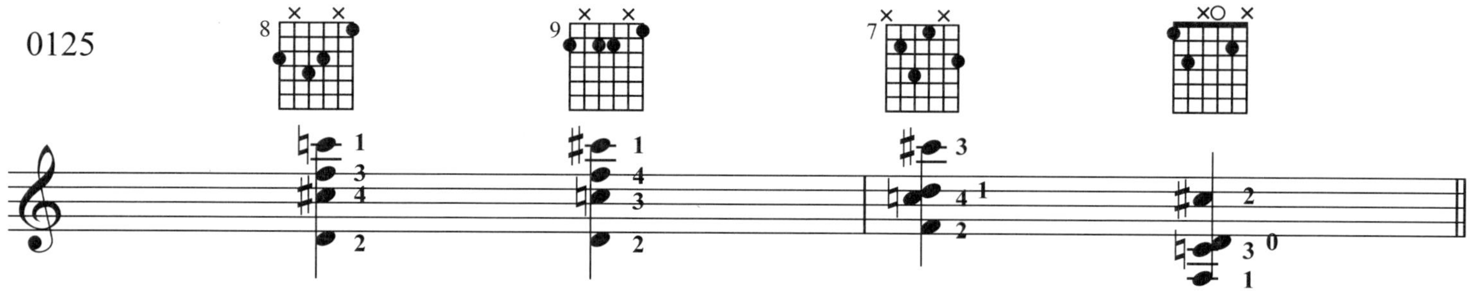

0126

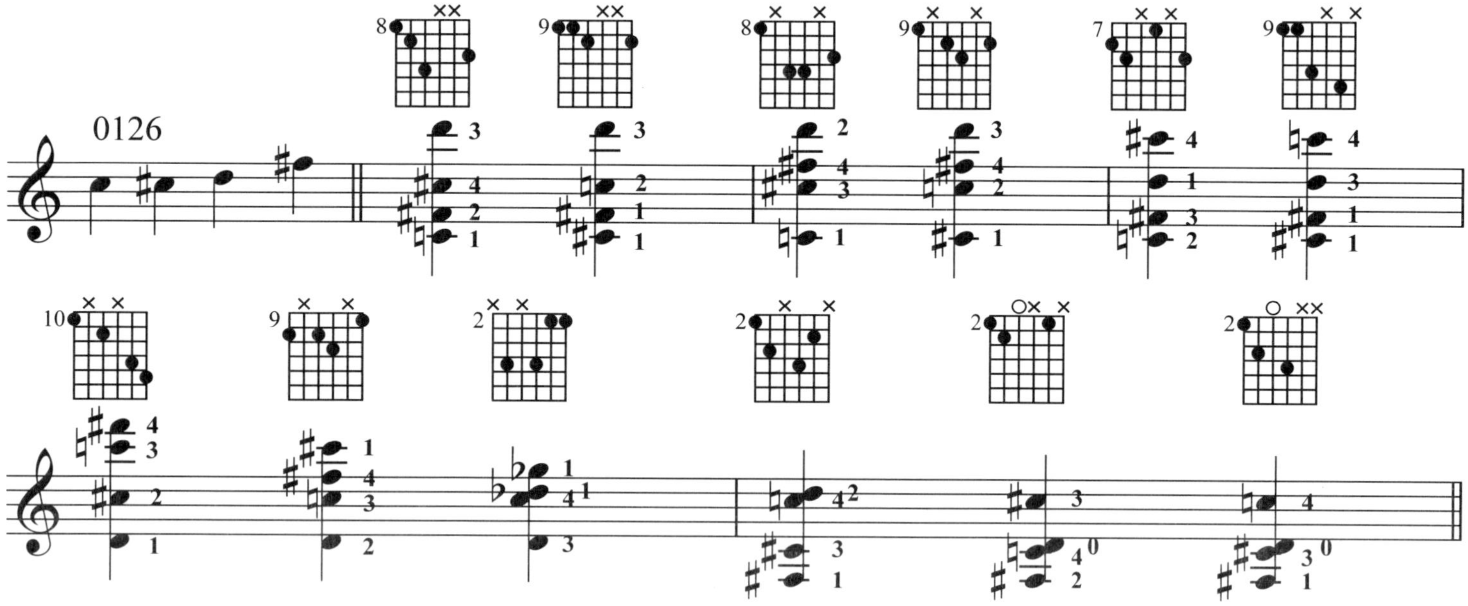

0127

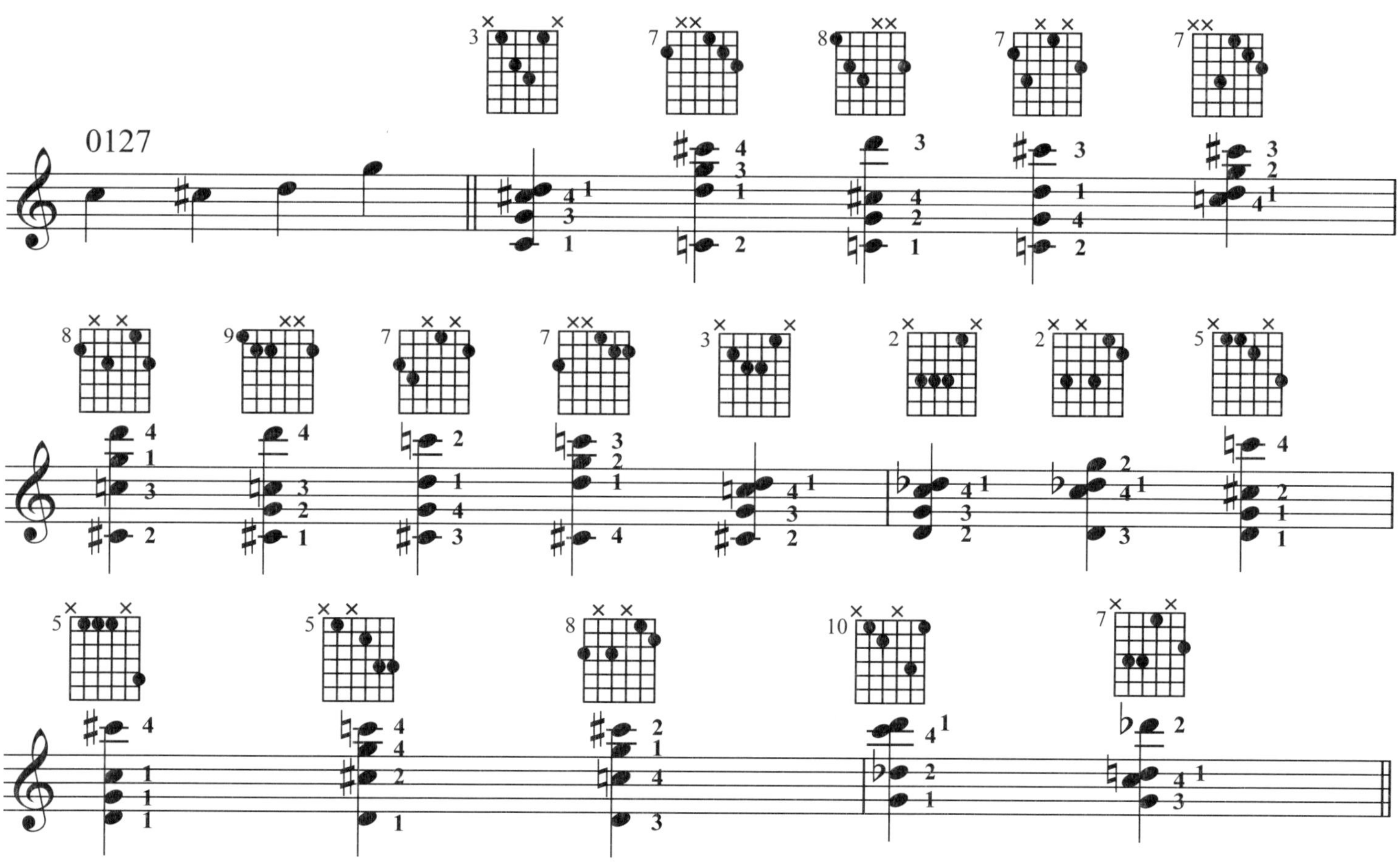

0134

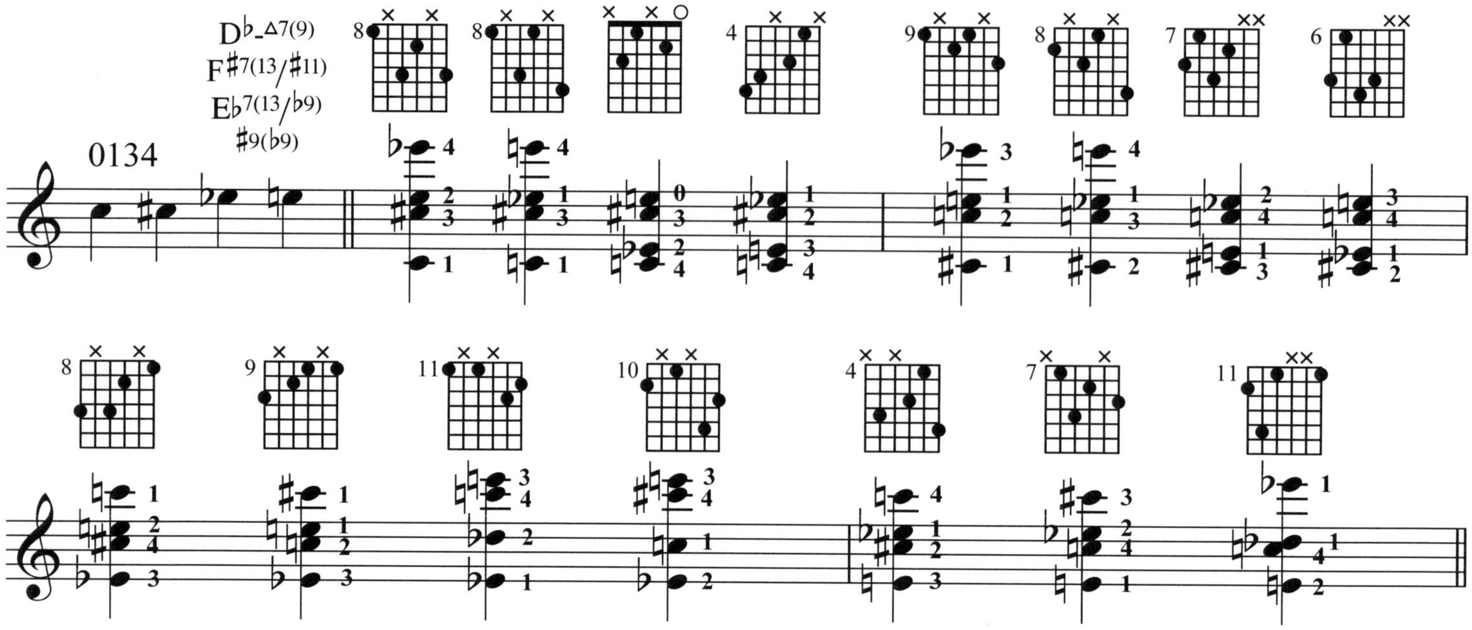

0135

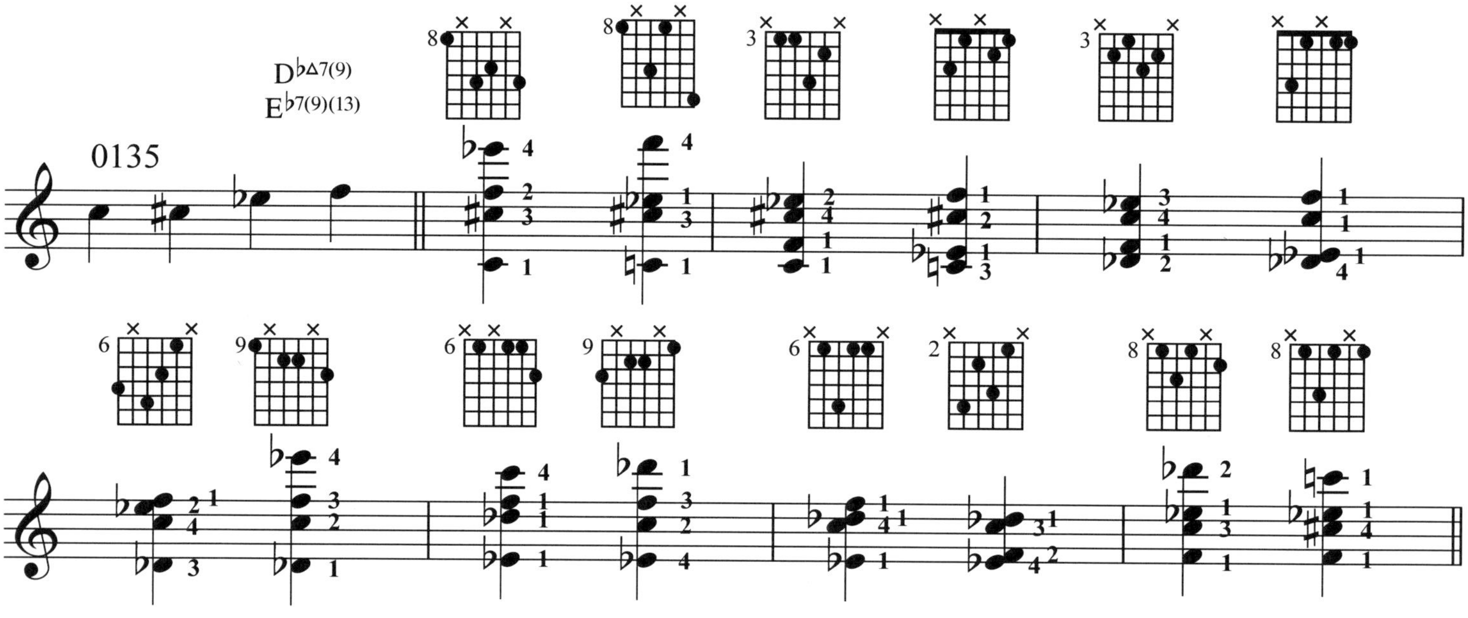

0136

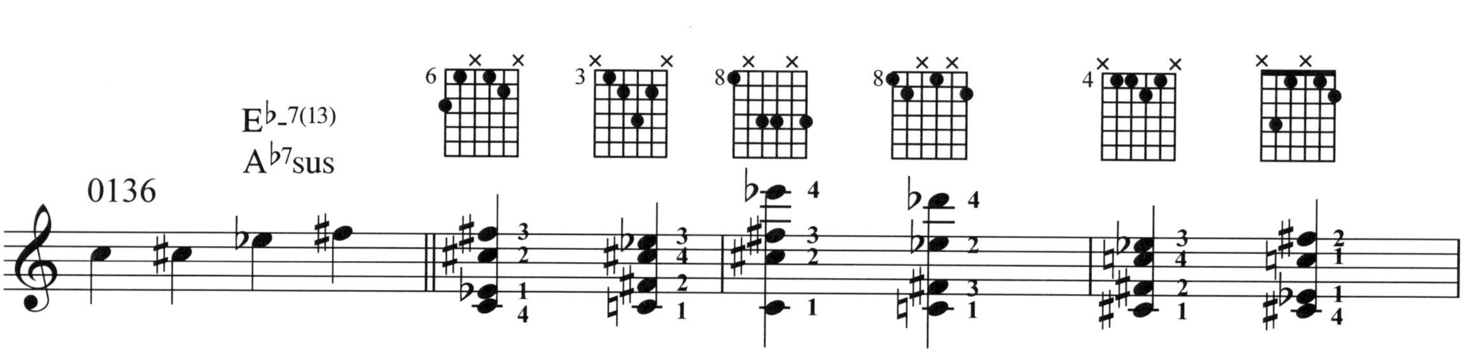

0136

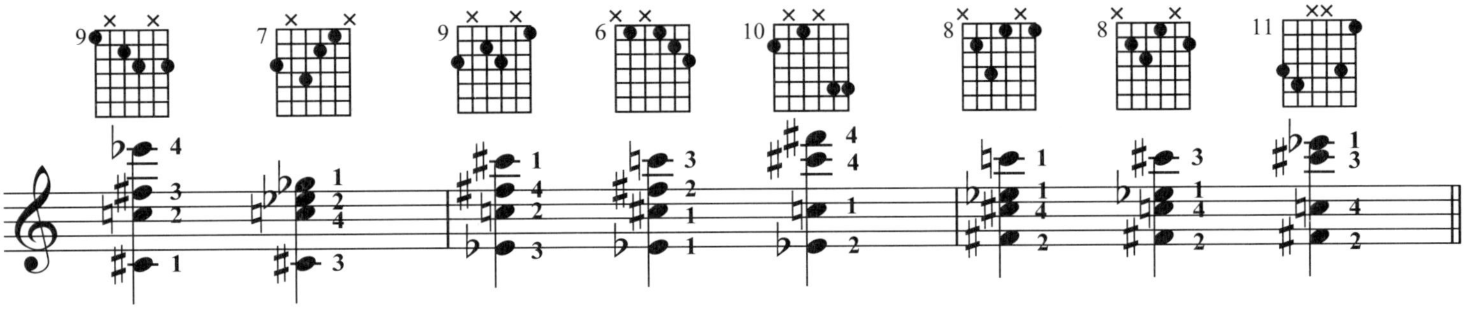

0137

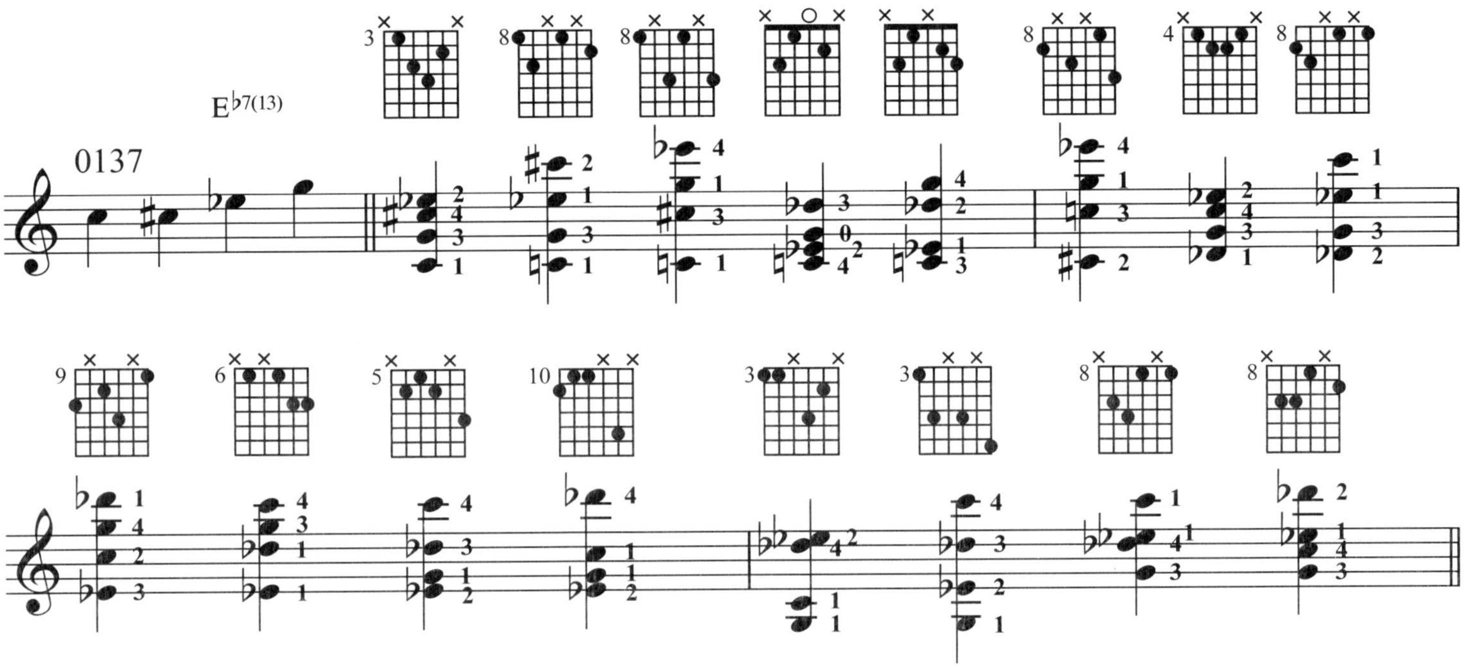

0145

0146
E♭7 13(♭9)
C/D♭
0147

0148
D♭-Δ7
0156
E♭-7(6/9)

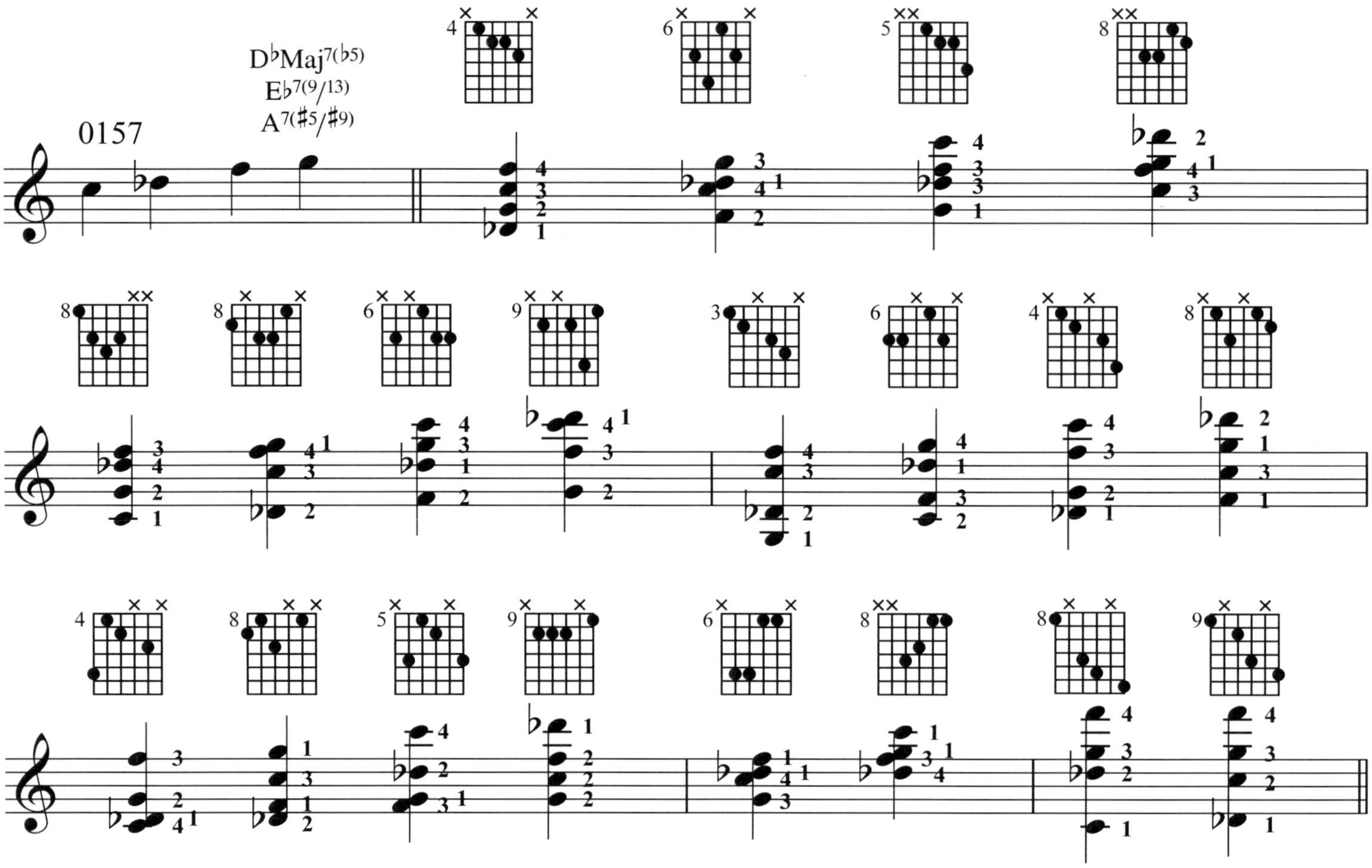
0157
D♭Maj7(♭5)
E♭7(9/13)
A7(♯5/♯9)

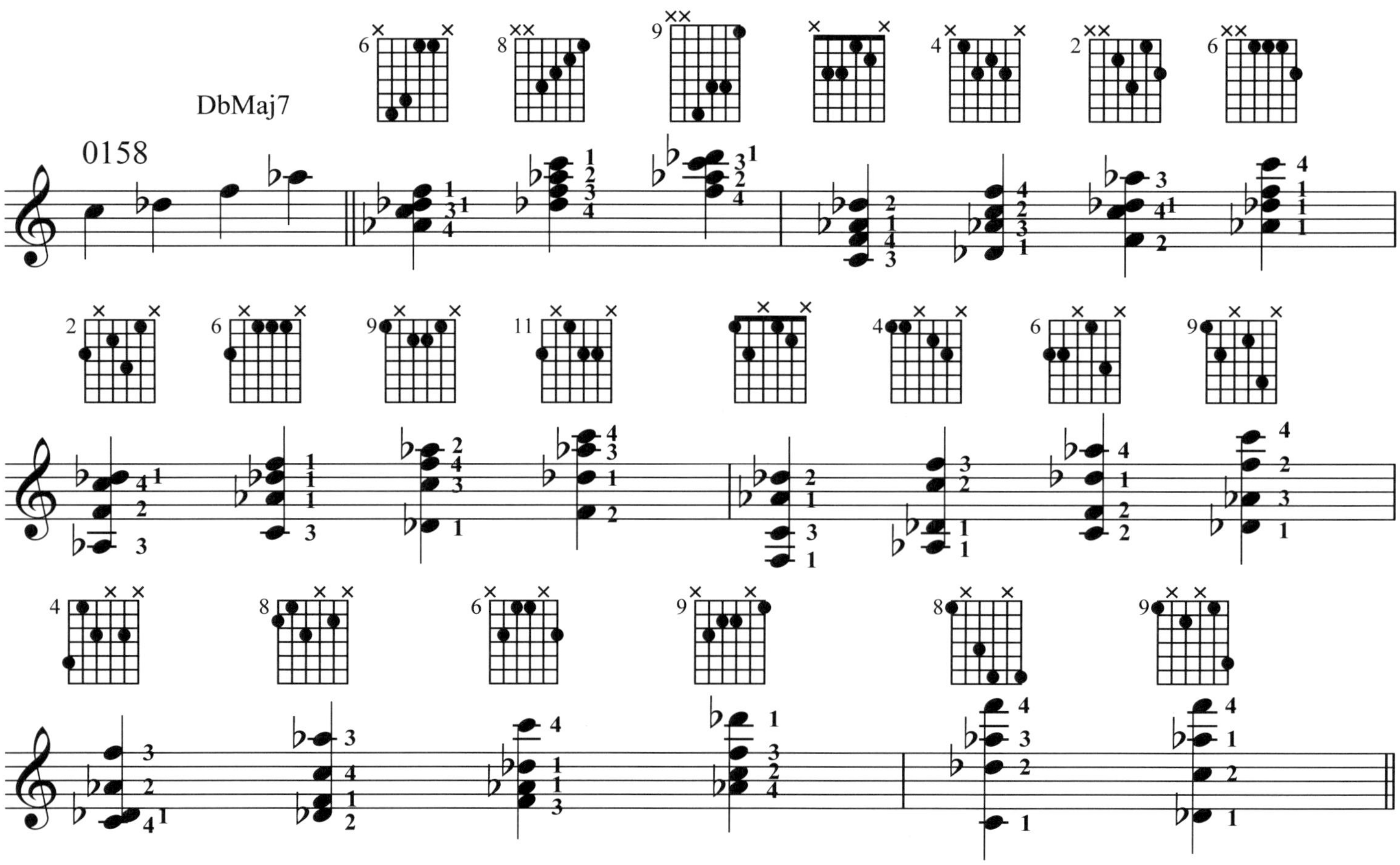
0158
DbMaj7

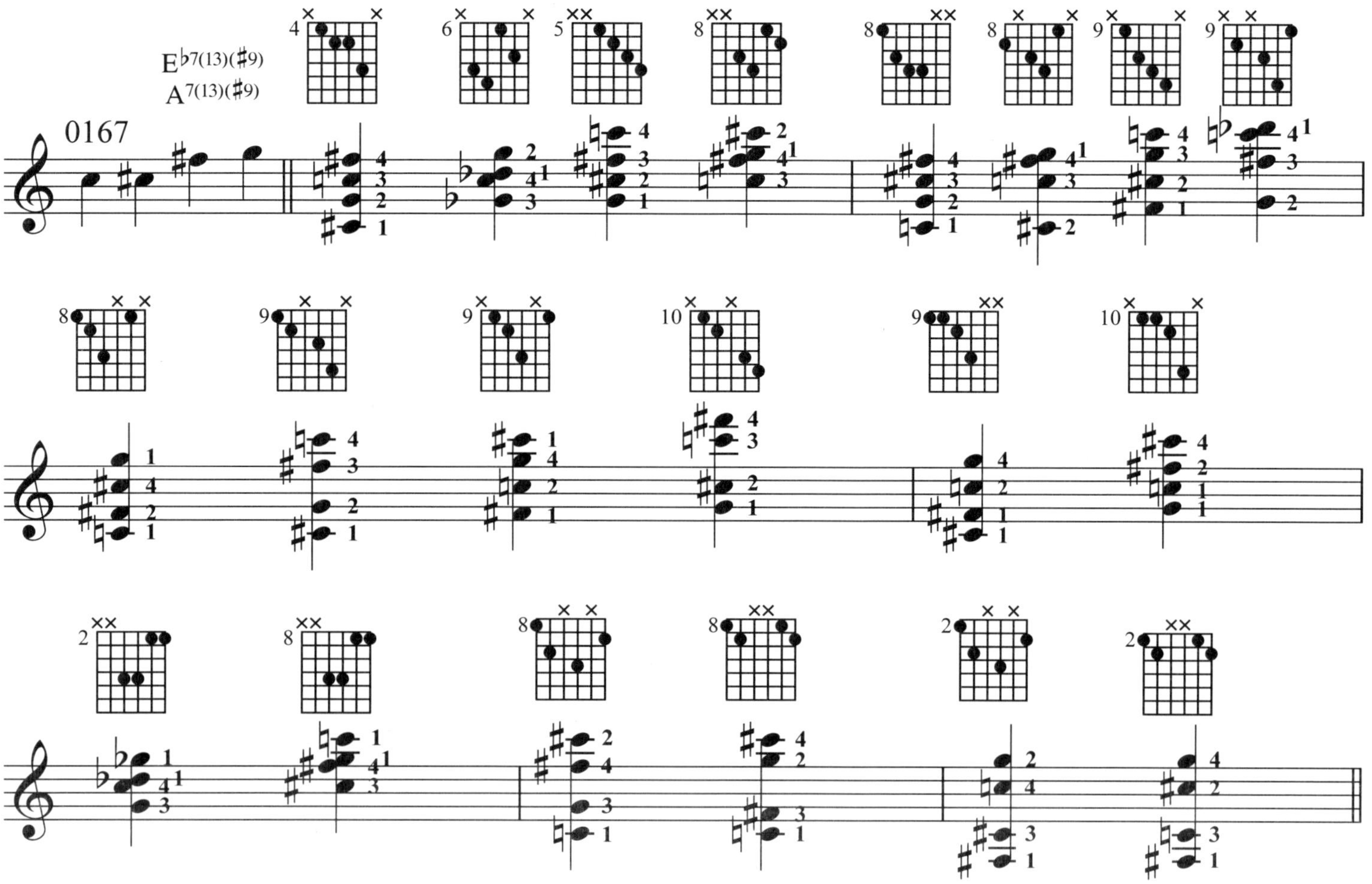
E♭7(13)(♯9)
A7(13)(♯9)
0167

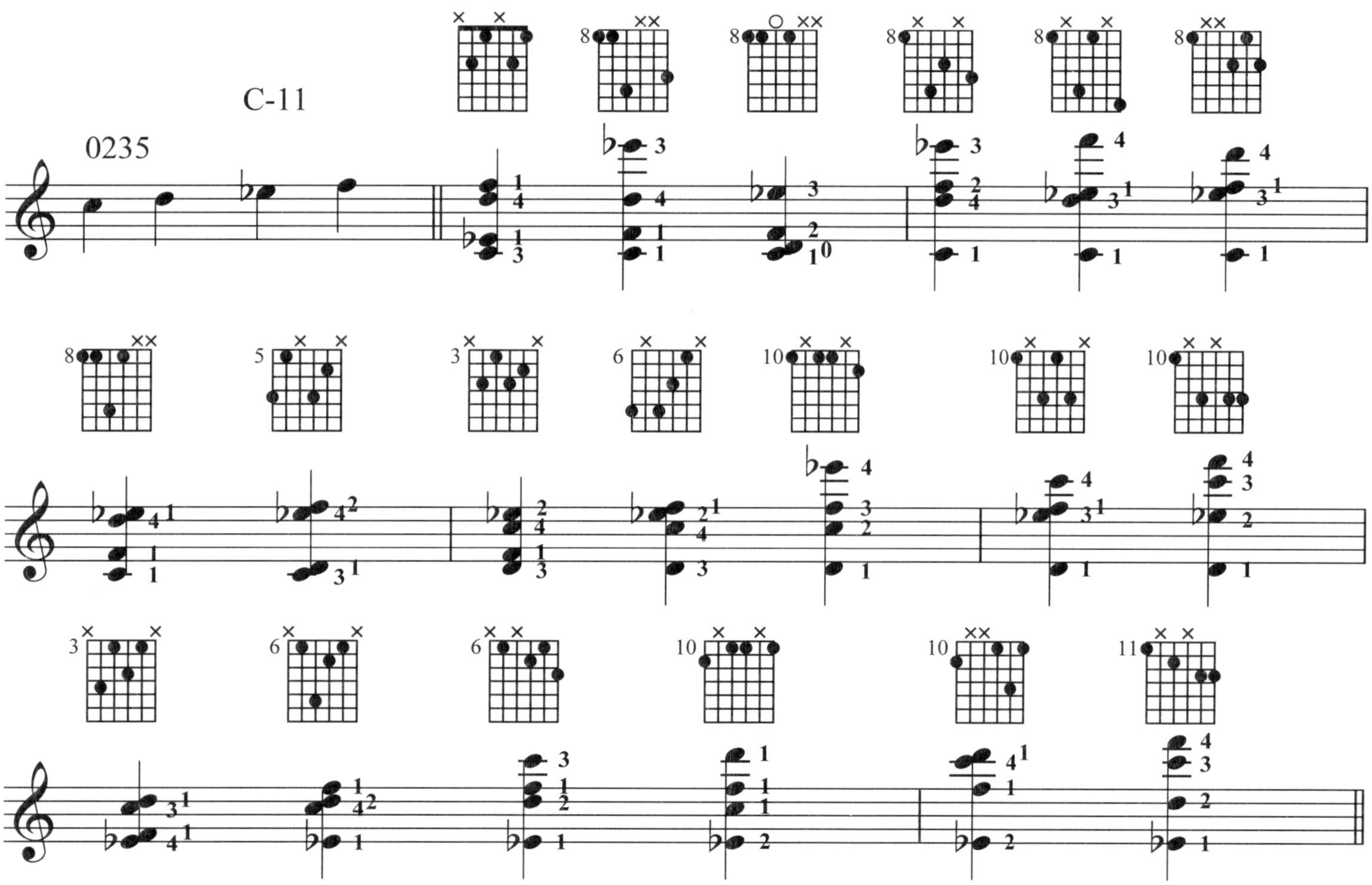
C-11
0235

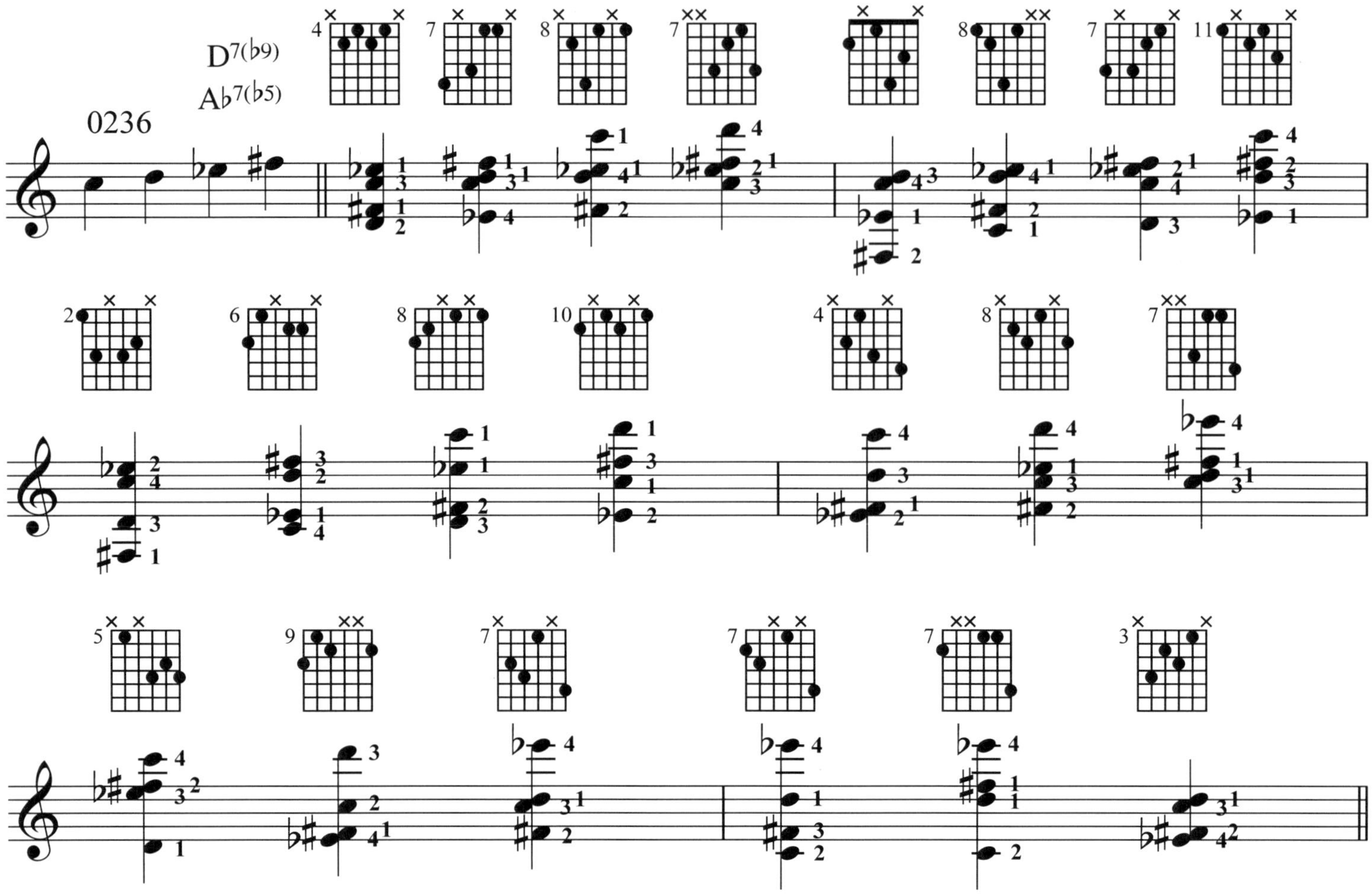
D7(♭9)
A♭7(♭5)
0236

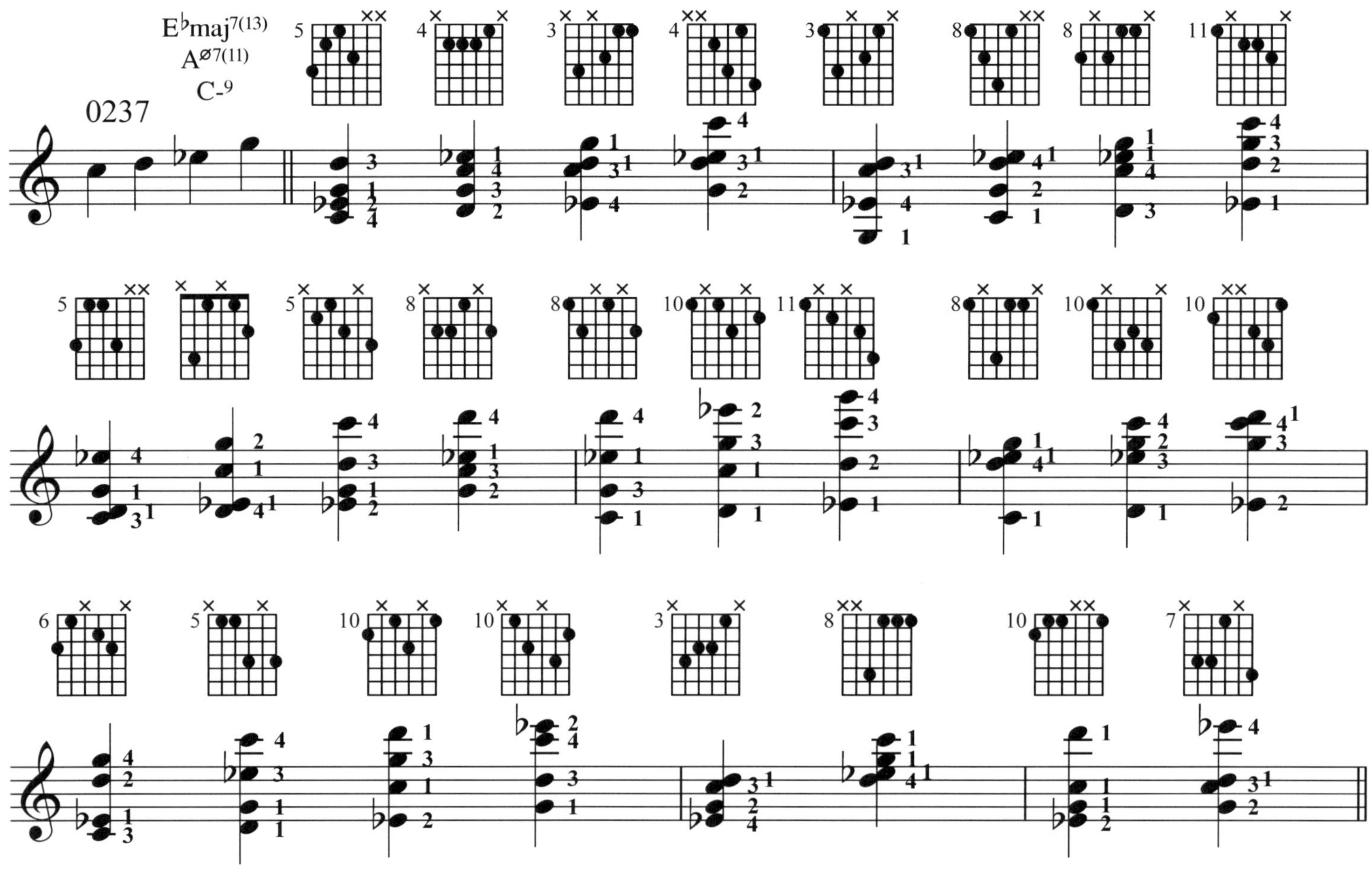
E♭maj7(13)
Aø7(11)
C-9
0237

D$^{7(9)}$

0246

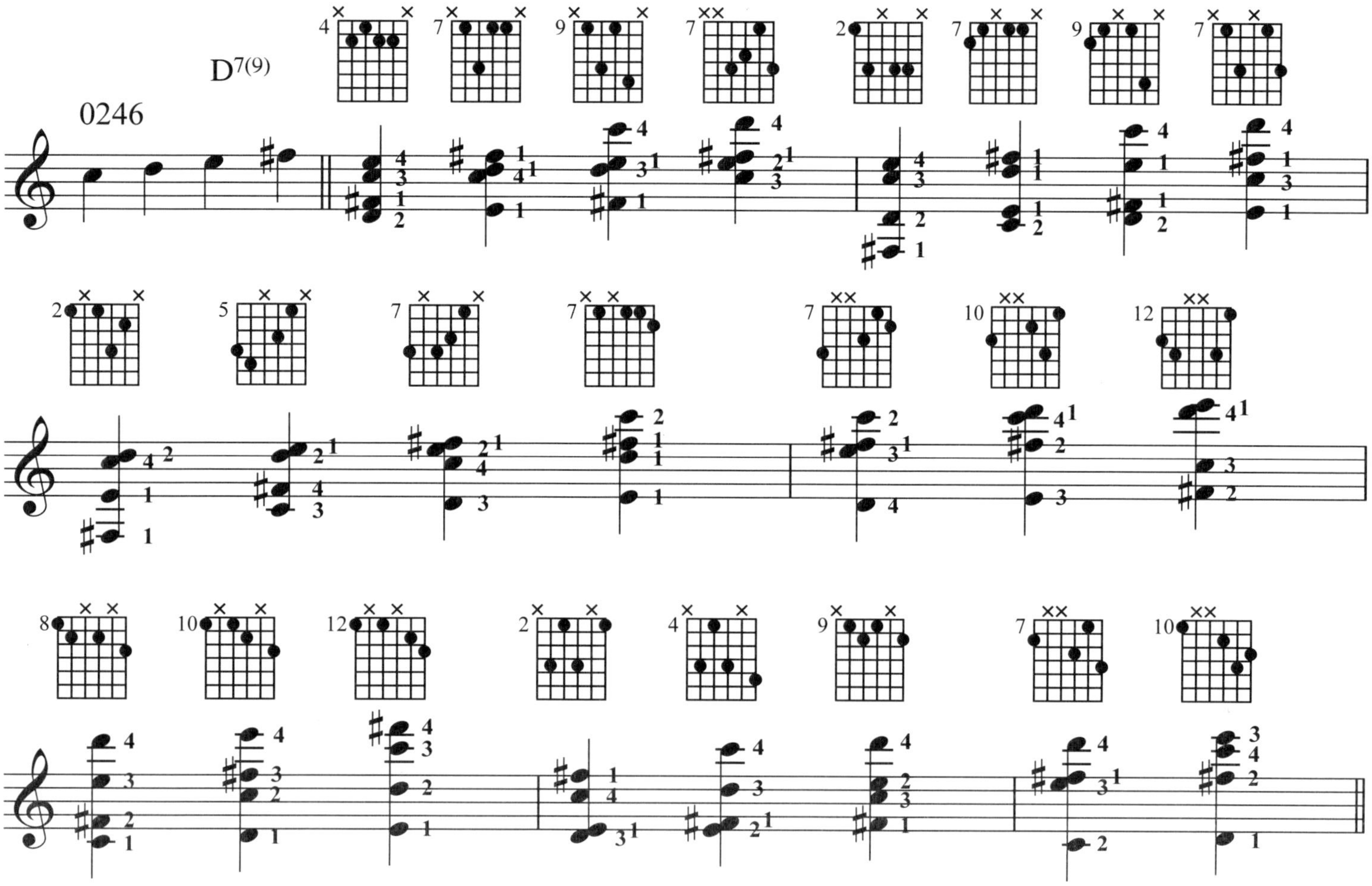

Cma^{9}
E-$^{7(\sharp 5)}$
C/D

0247

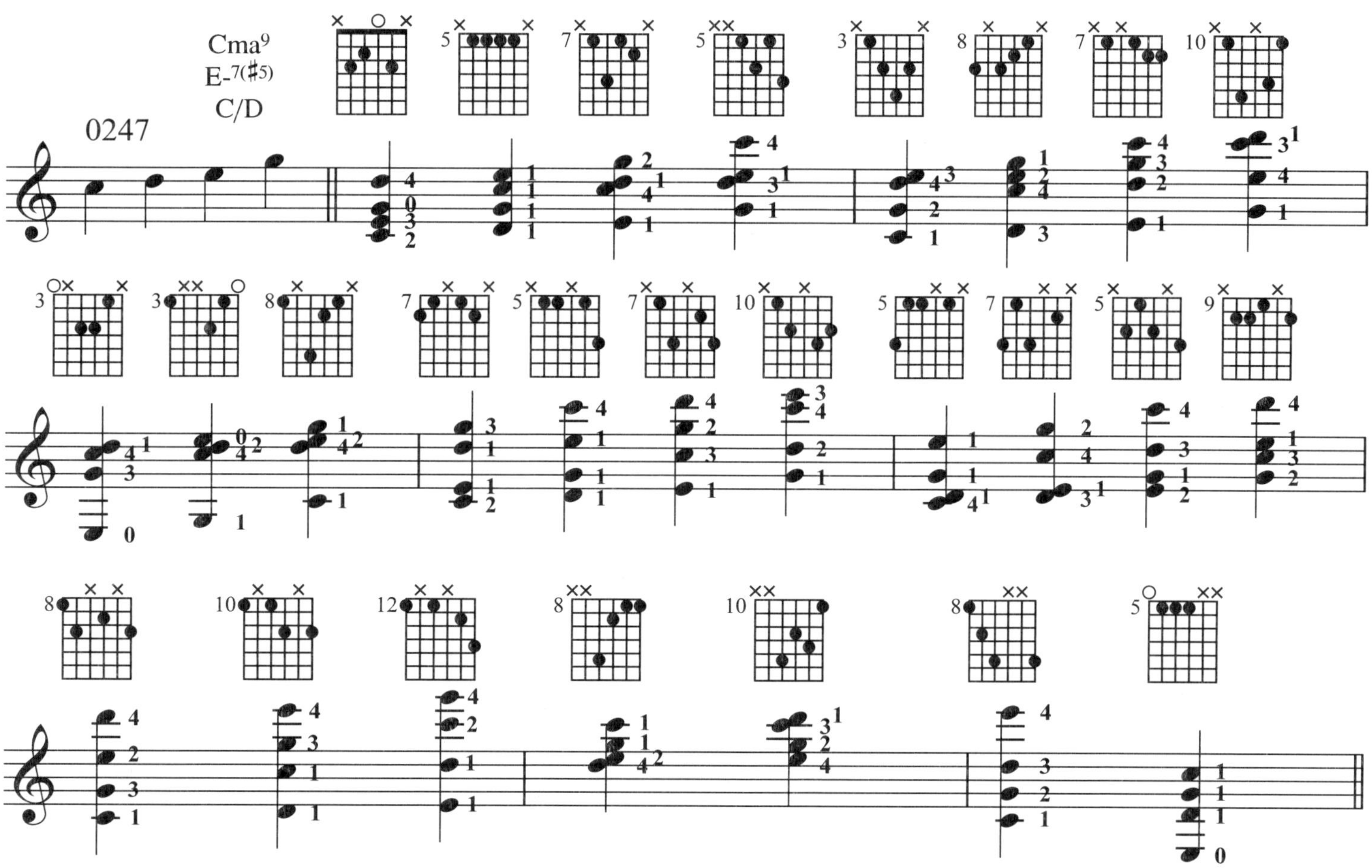

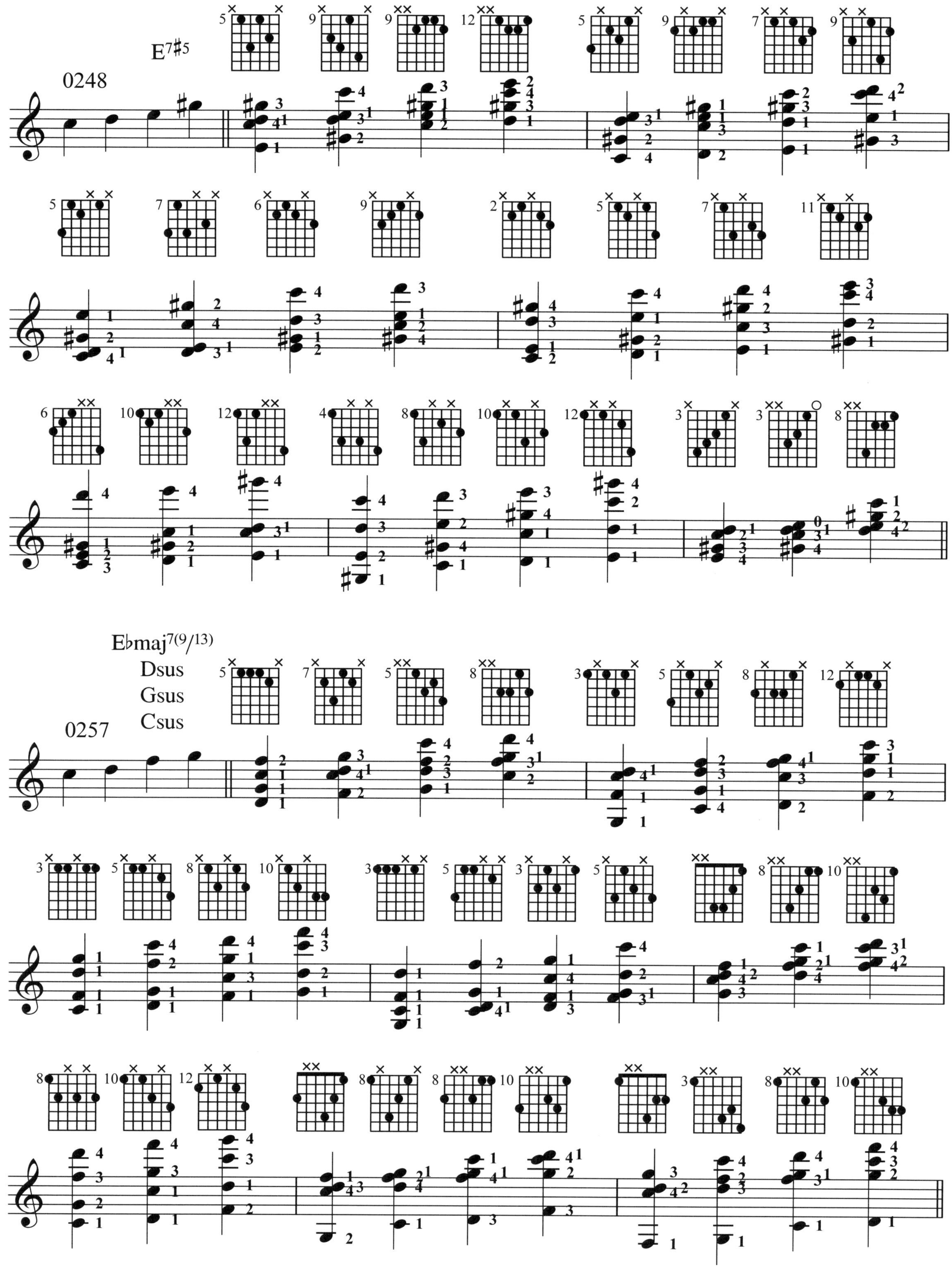
E7♯5
0248
E♭maj7(9/13)
Dsus
Gsus
Csus
0257

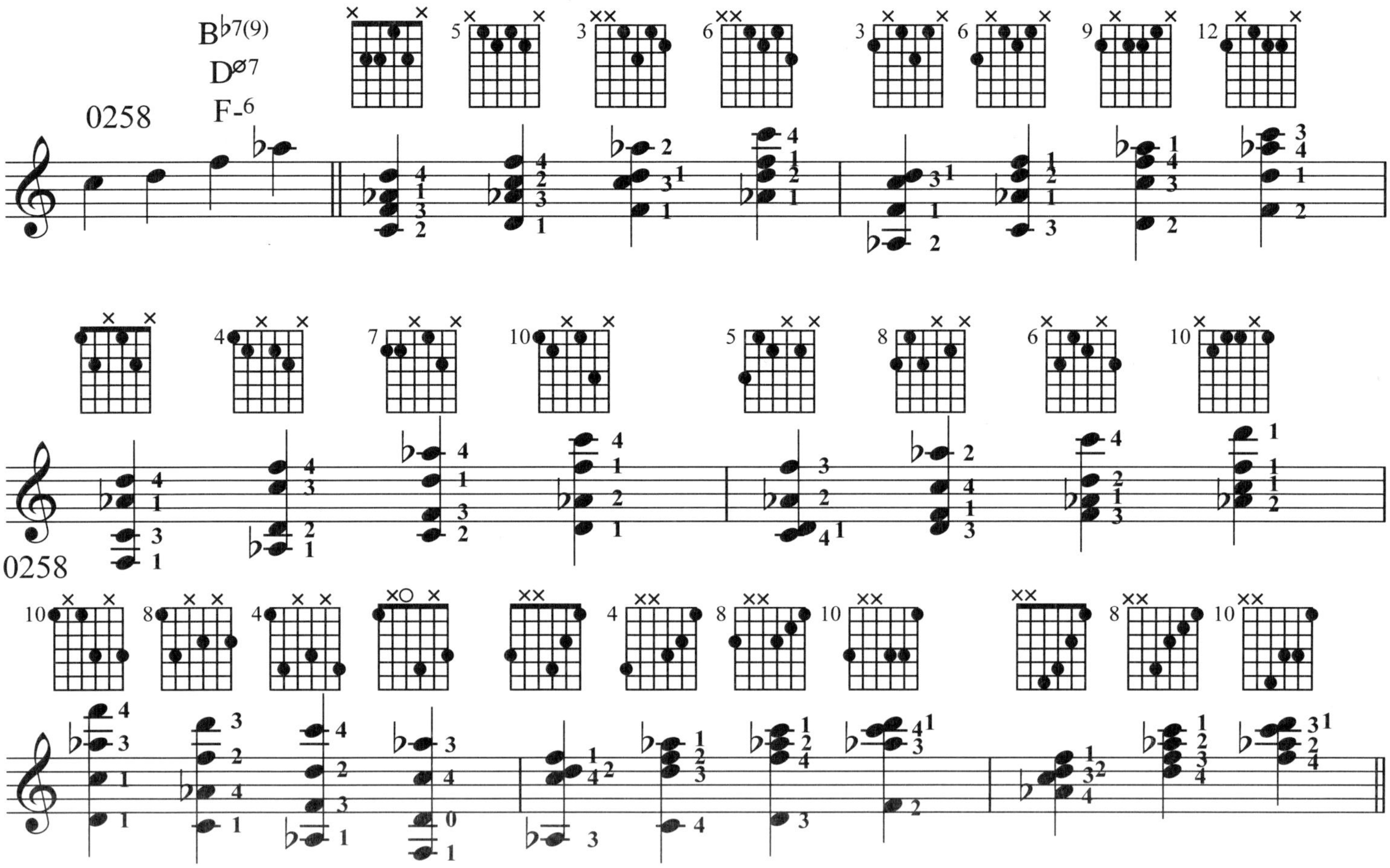
0258
B♭7(9)
Dø7
F-6
0258

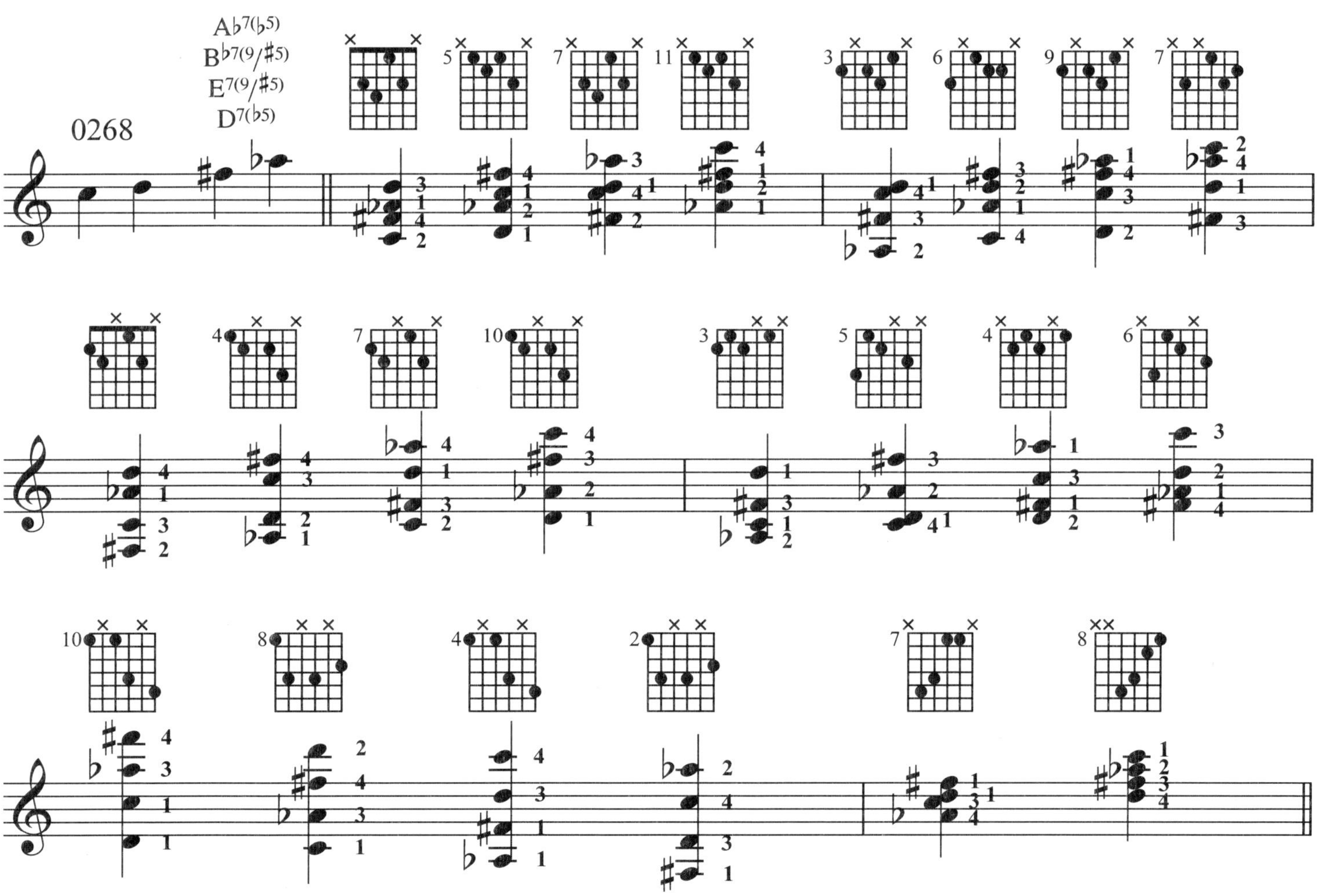
0268
A♭7(♭5)
B♭7(9/♯5)
E7(9/♯5)
D7(♭5)

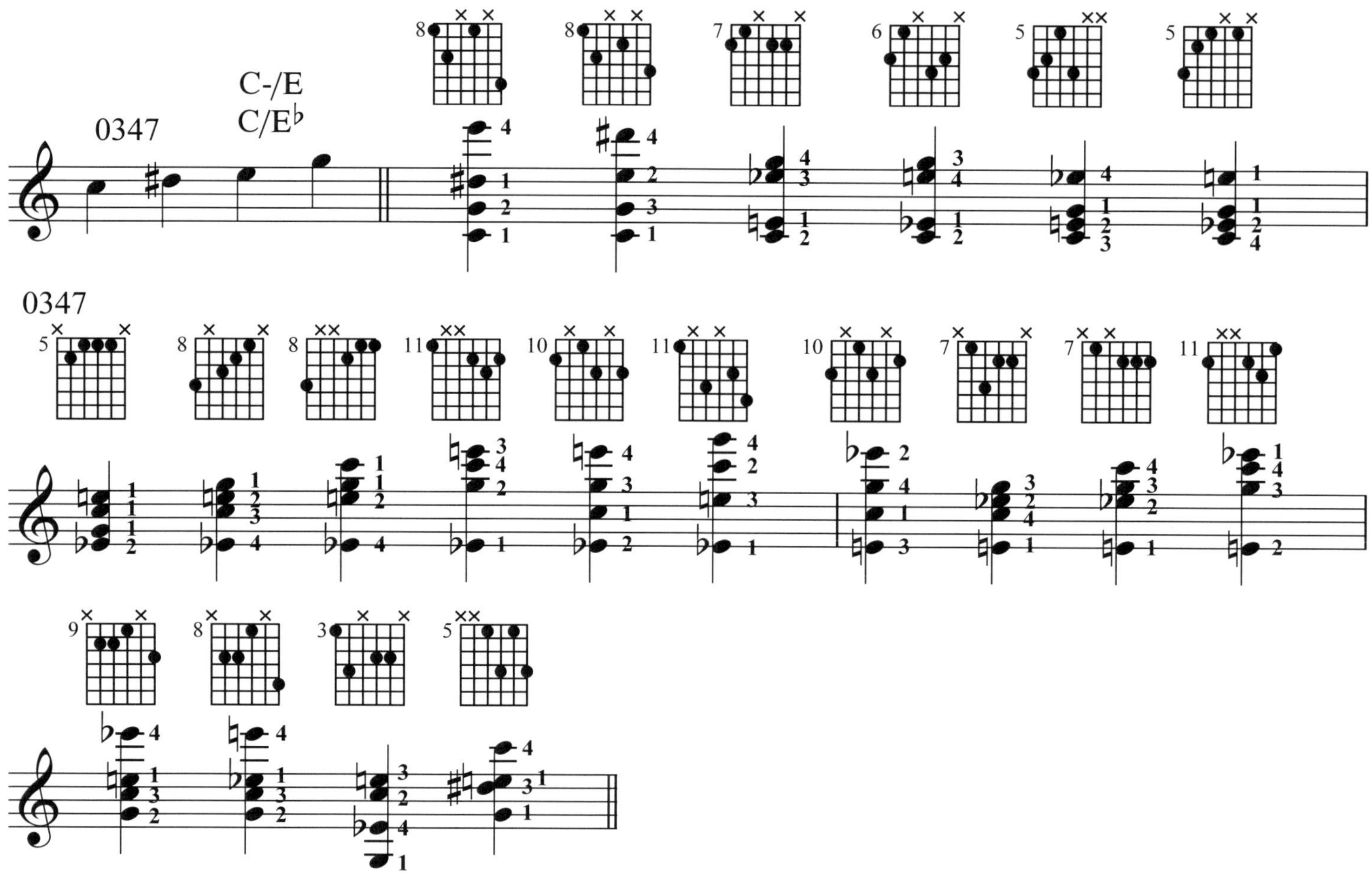
0347
C-/E
C/E♭
0347

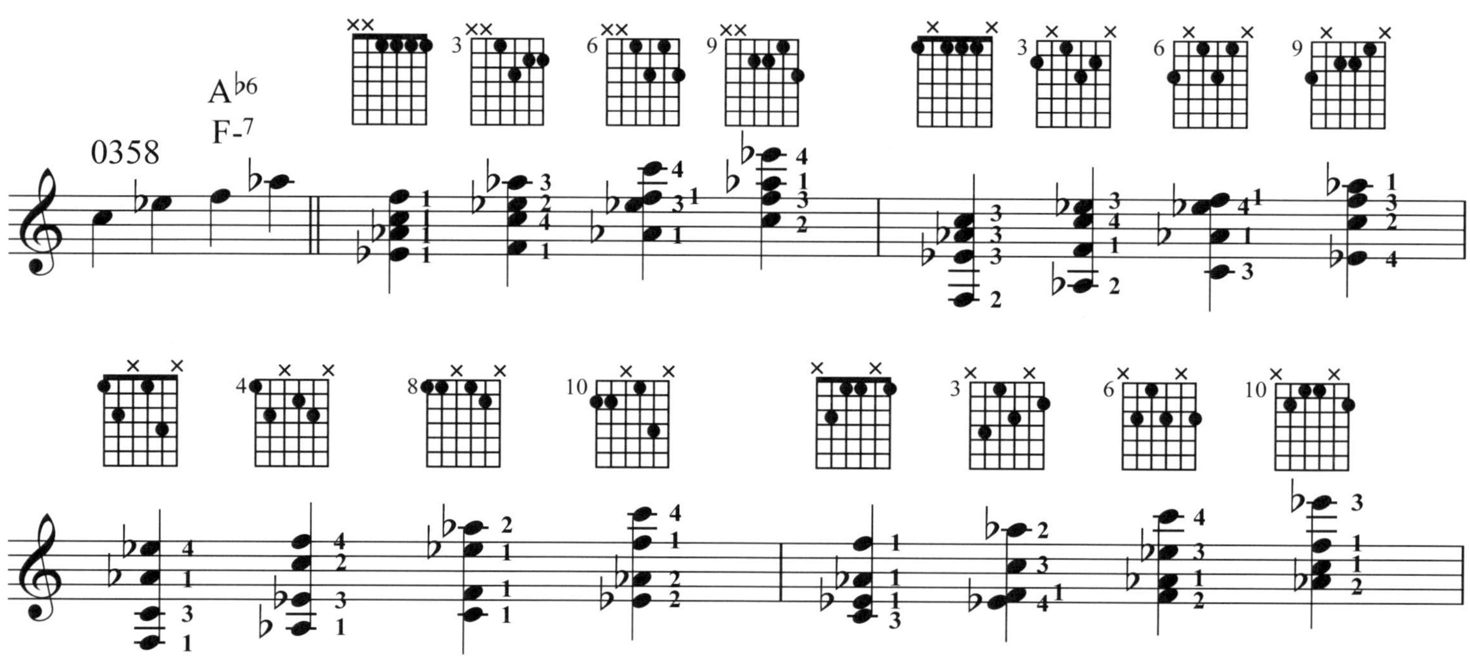
0358
A♭6
F-7

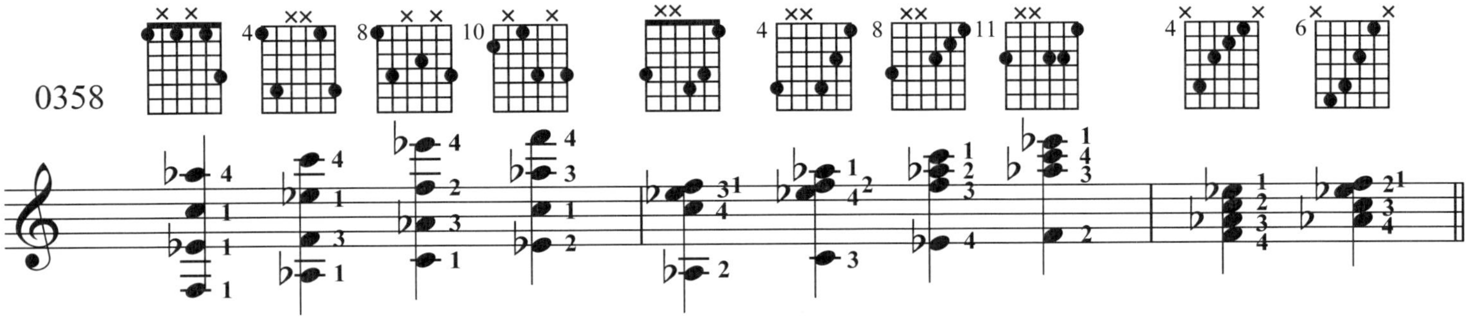
0358

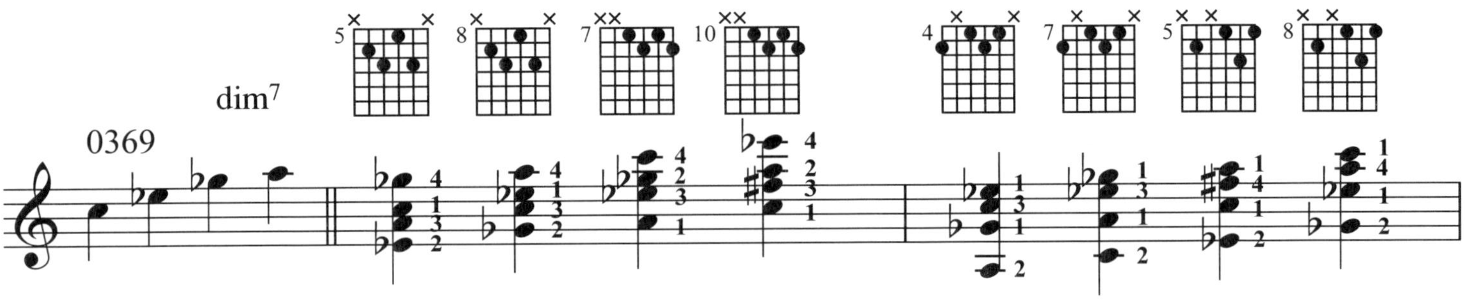
dim7
0369

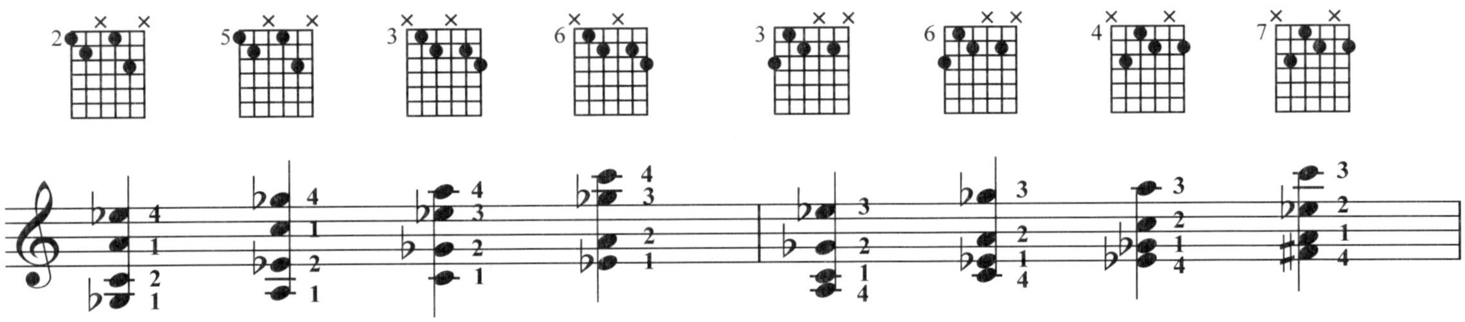

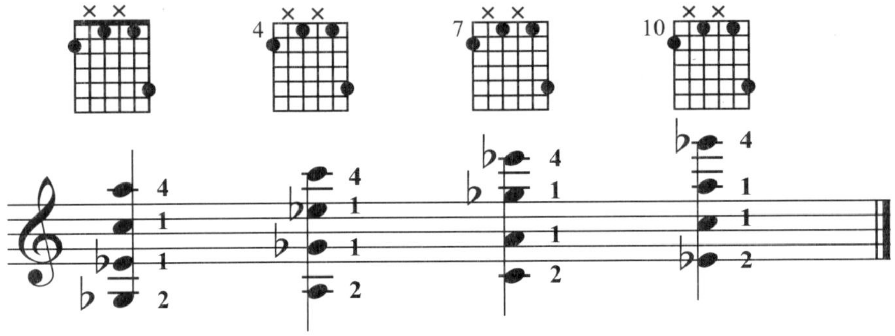

Inverted Tetra-Chords

Inverted Tetra-Chords

Symmetrical (same as 0123, previous section)

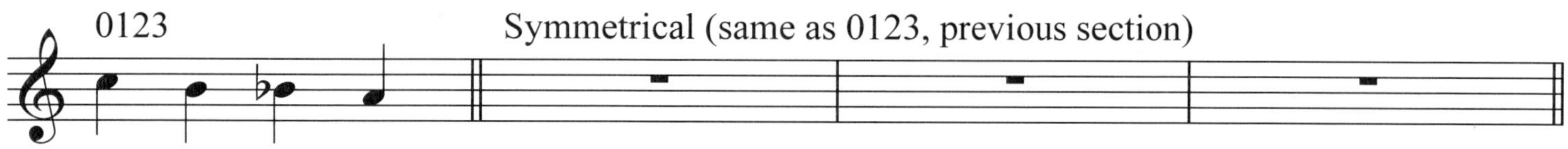

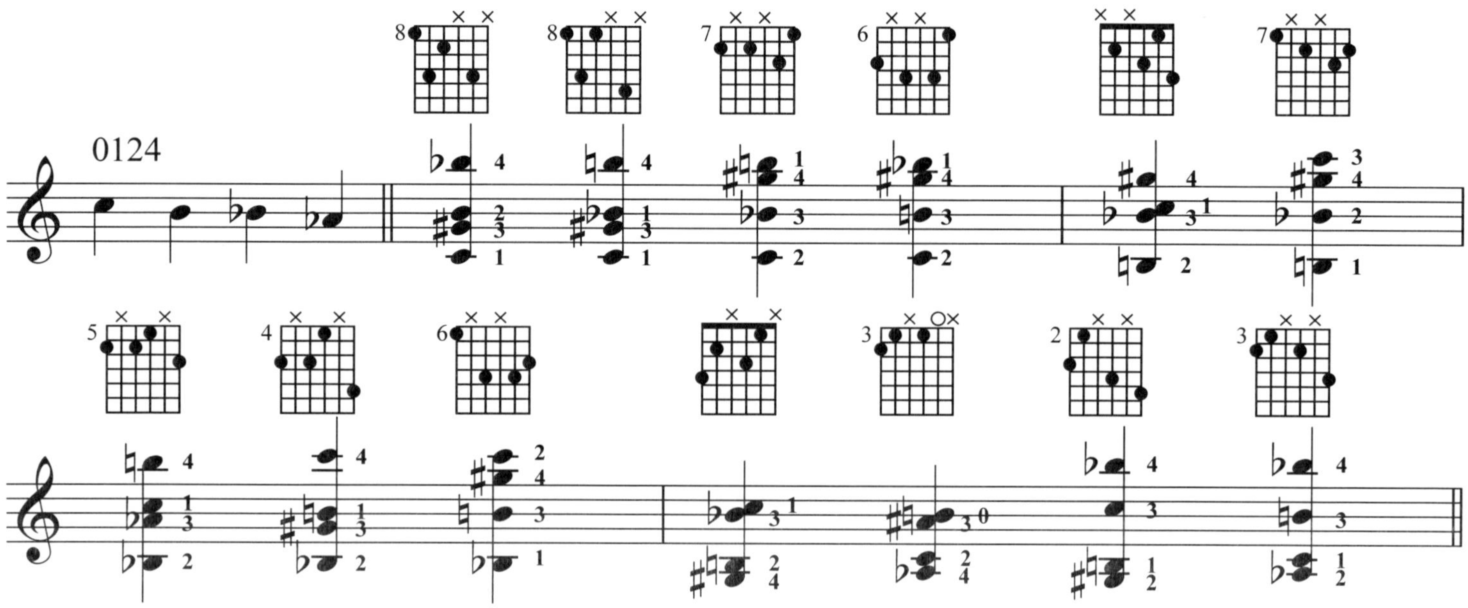

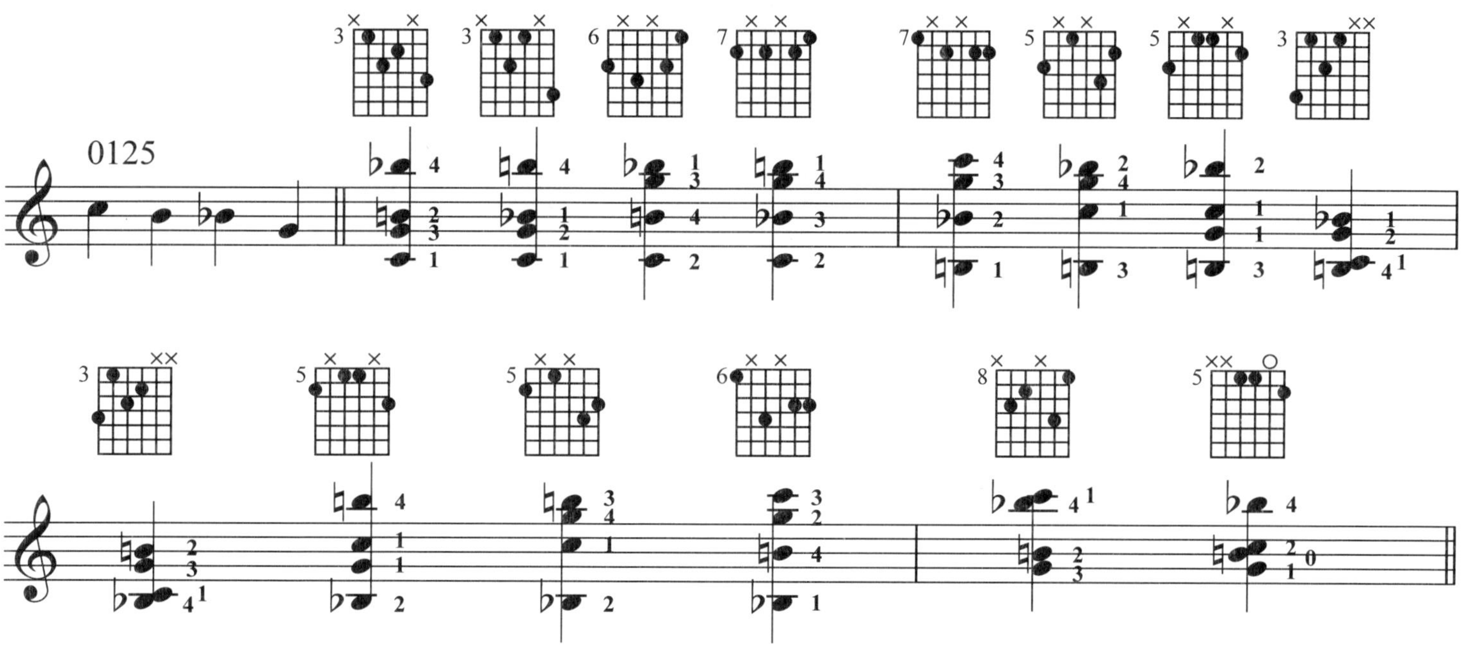

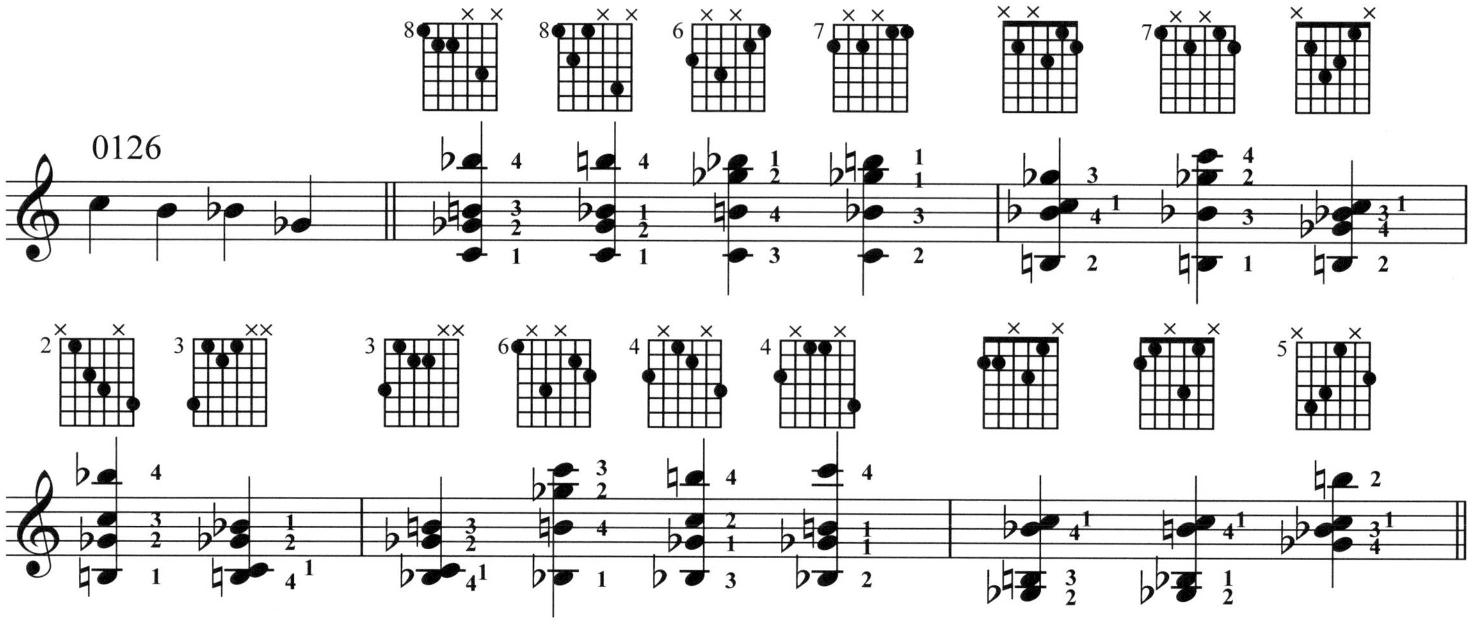
0126

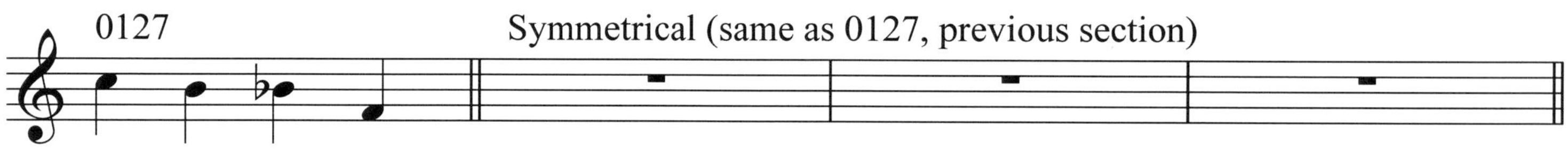
0127
Symmetrical (same as 0127, previous section)

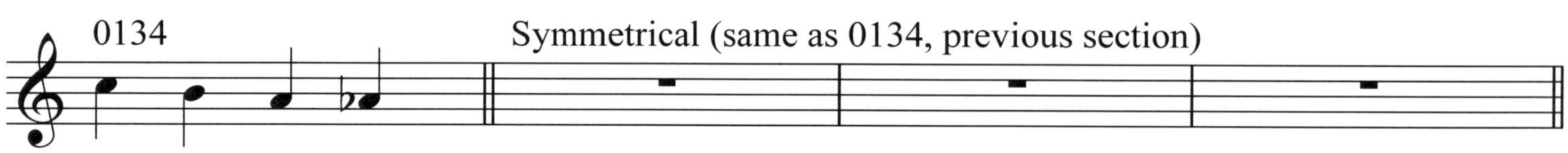
0134
Symmetrical (same as 0134, previous section)

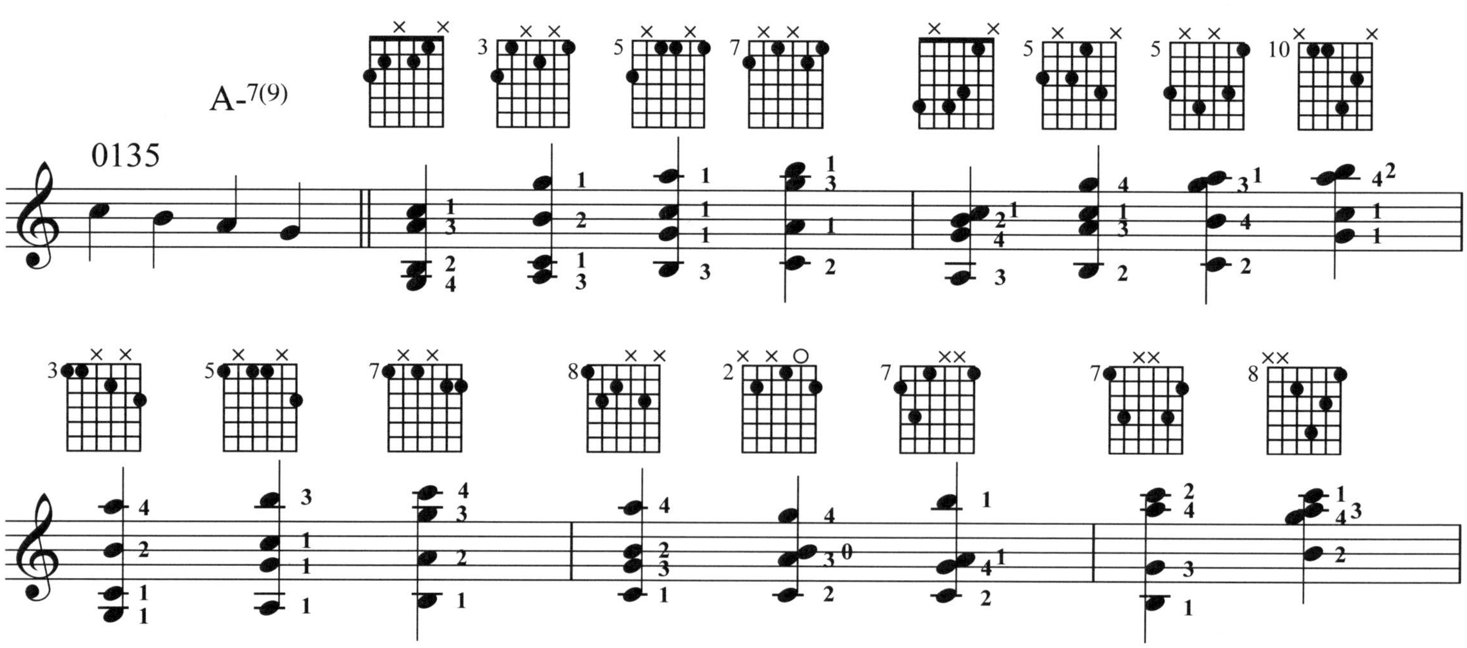
A-7(9)
0135

0135

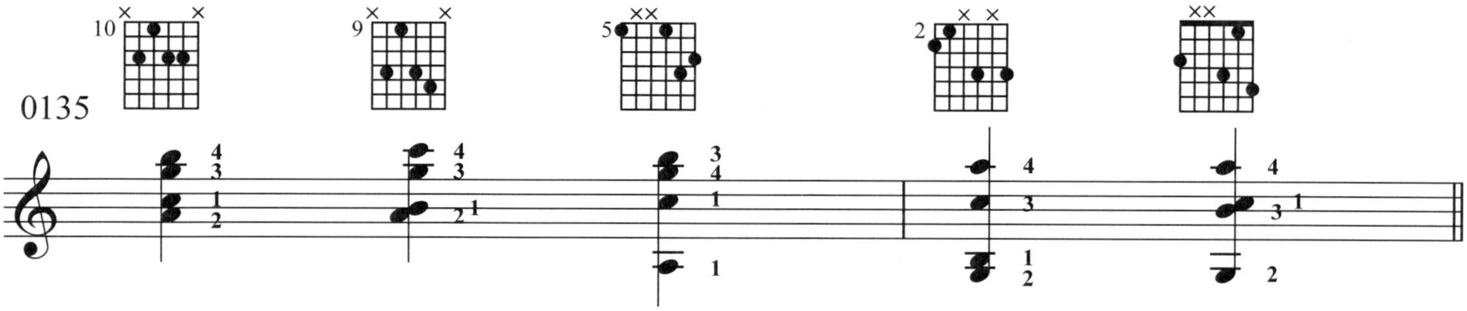

0136

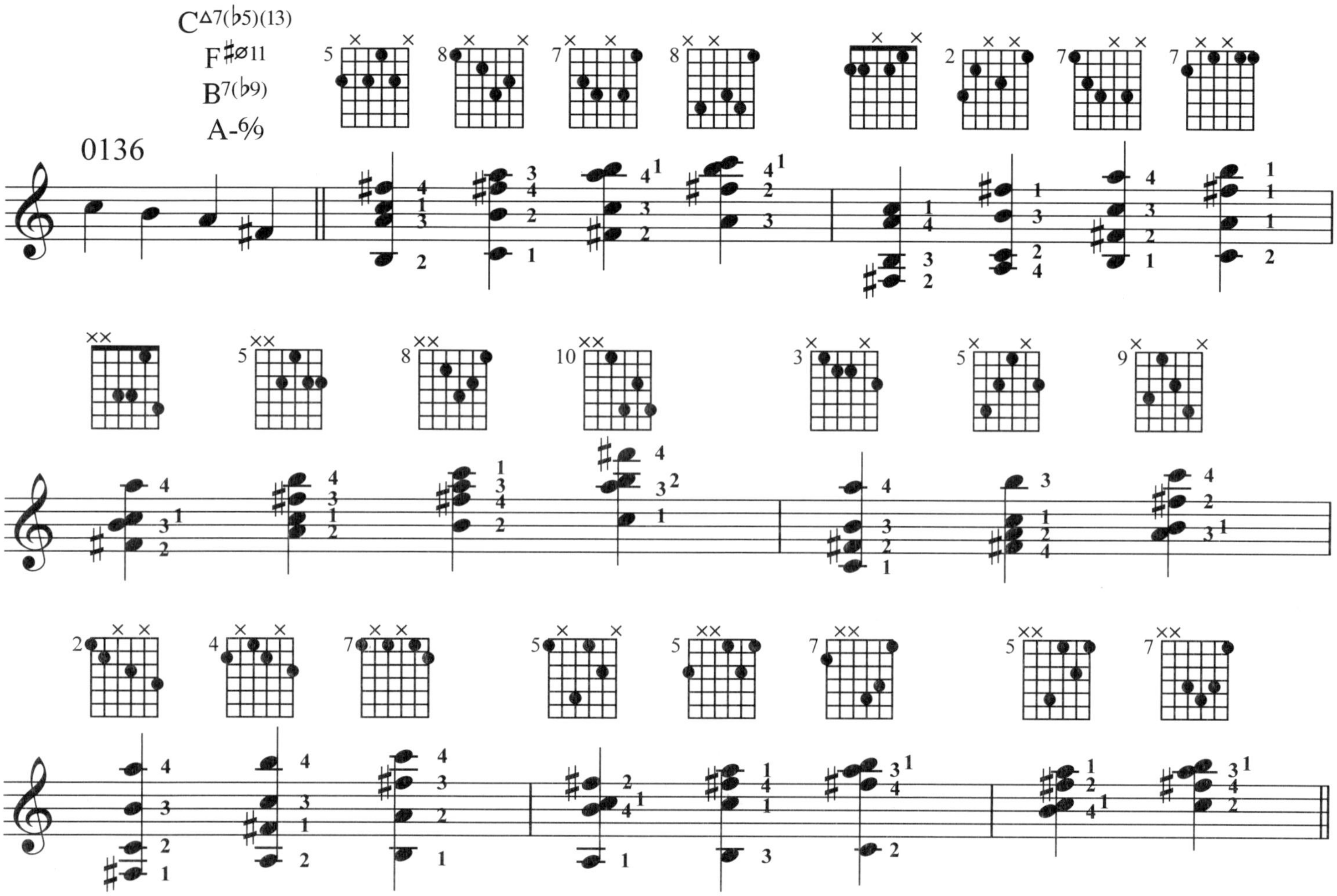

0137

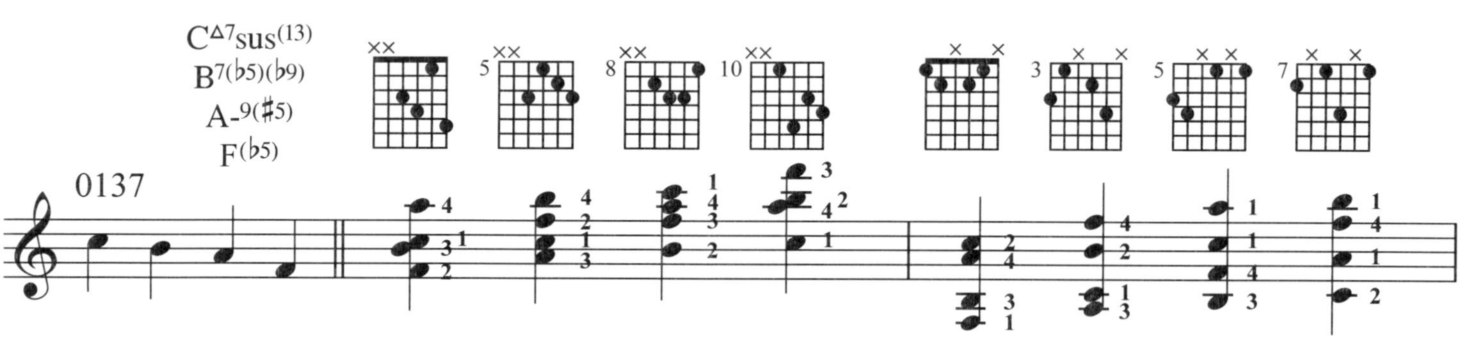

0137

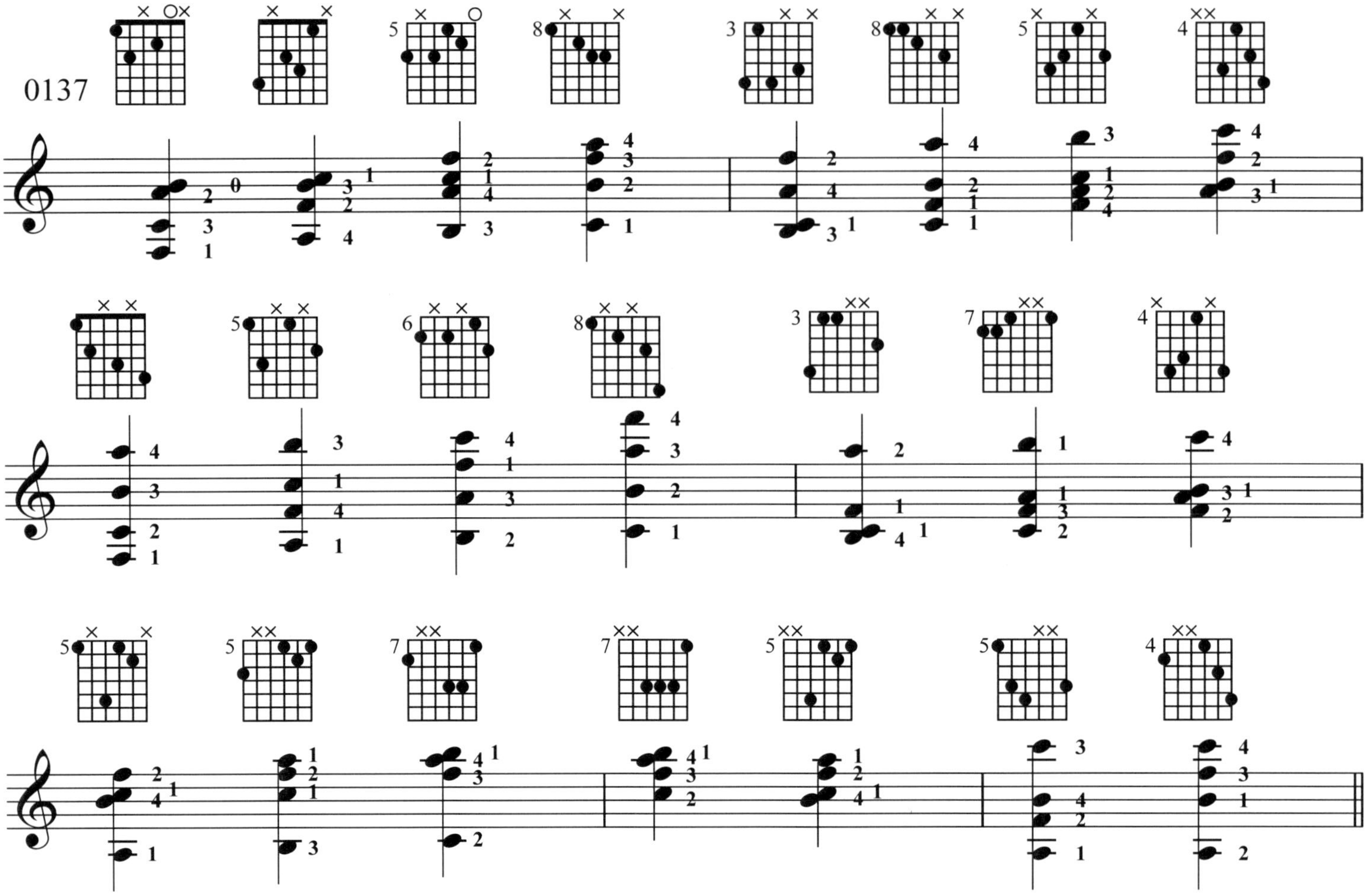

0145

Symmetrical (same as 0145, previous section)

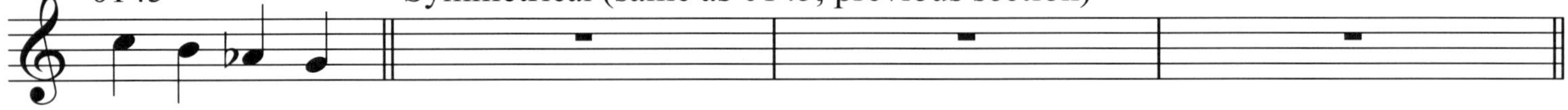

A♭7(♯9)

0146

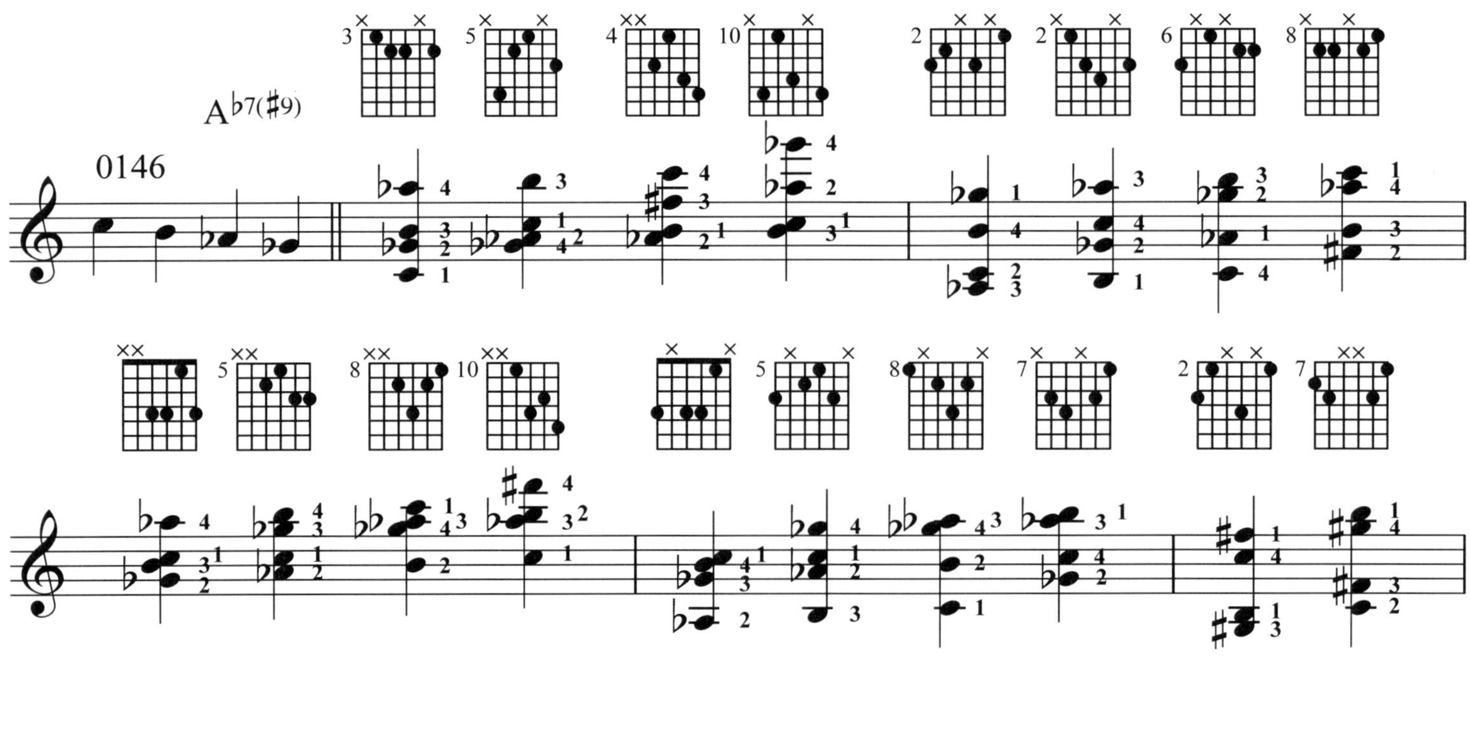

0146

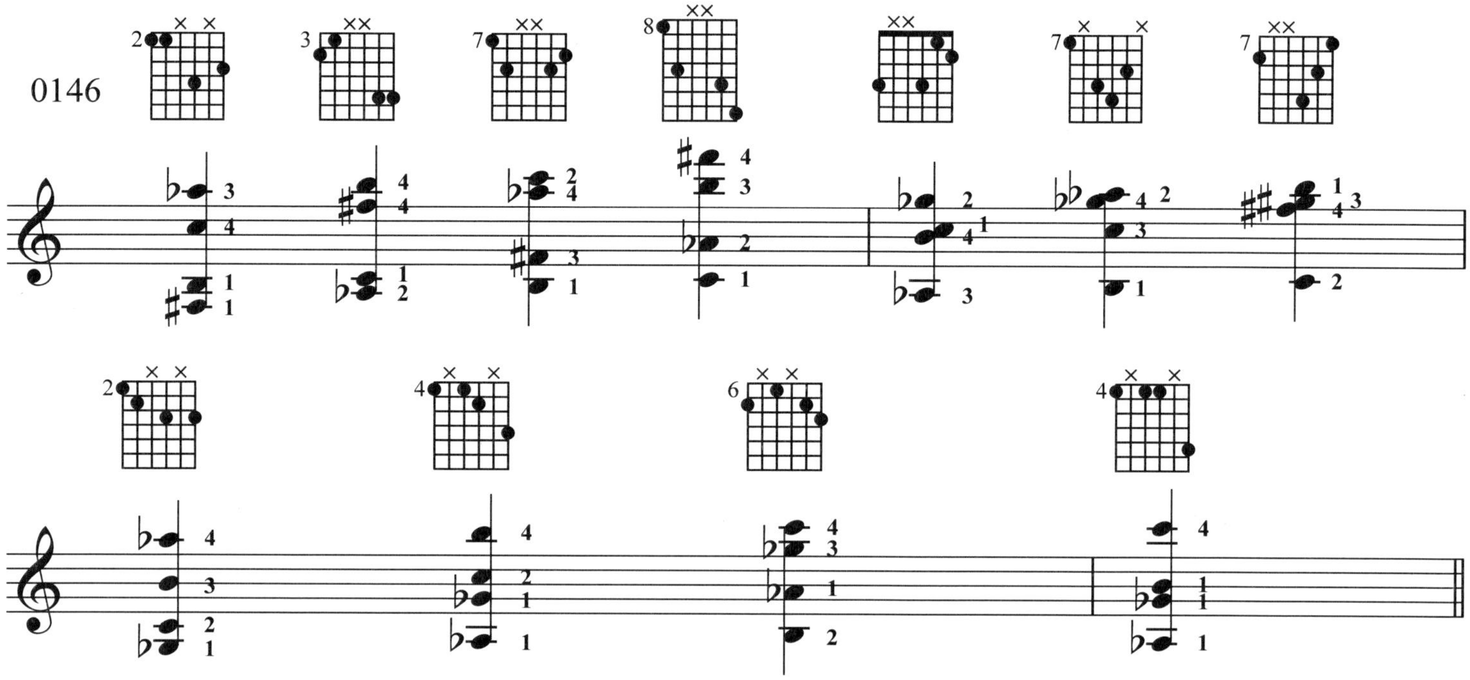

$C^{\Delta 7}sus^{(\sharp 5)}$
$F_{-}^{(\flat 5)}$

0147

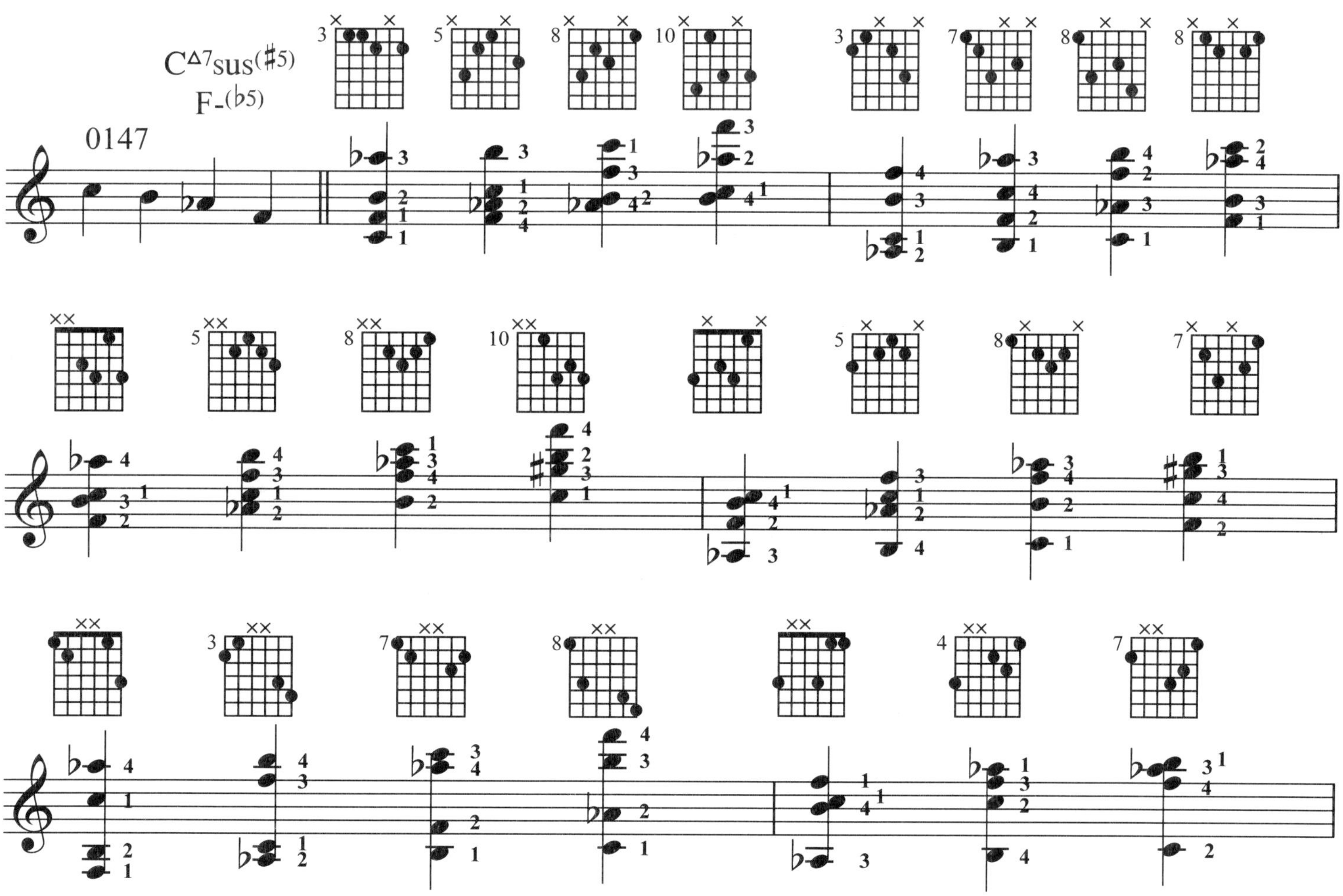

0147

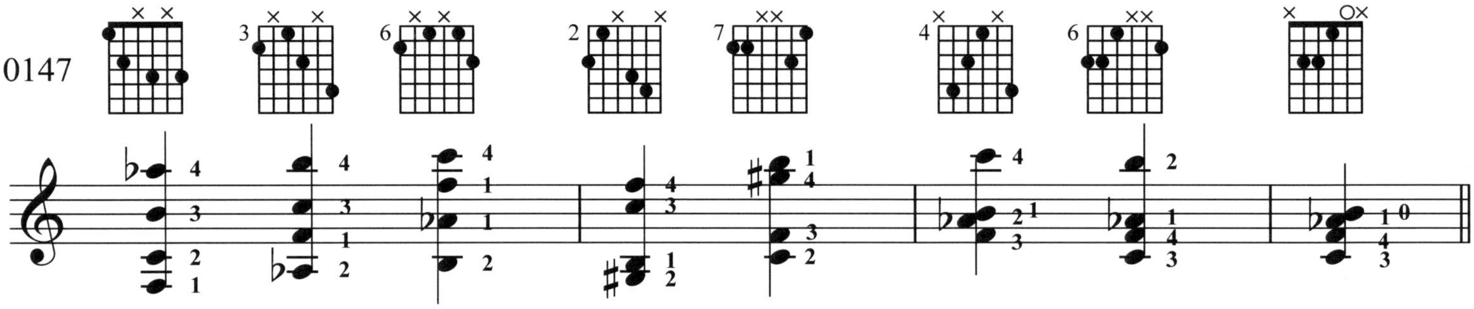

C$^{\Delta 7(\sharp 5)}$

0148

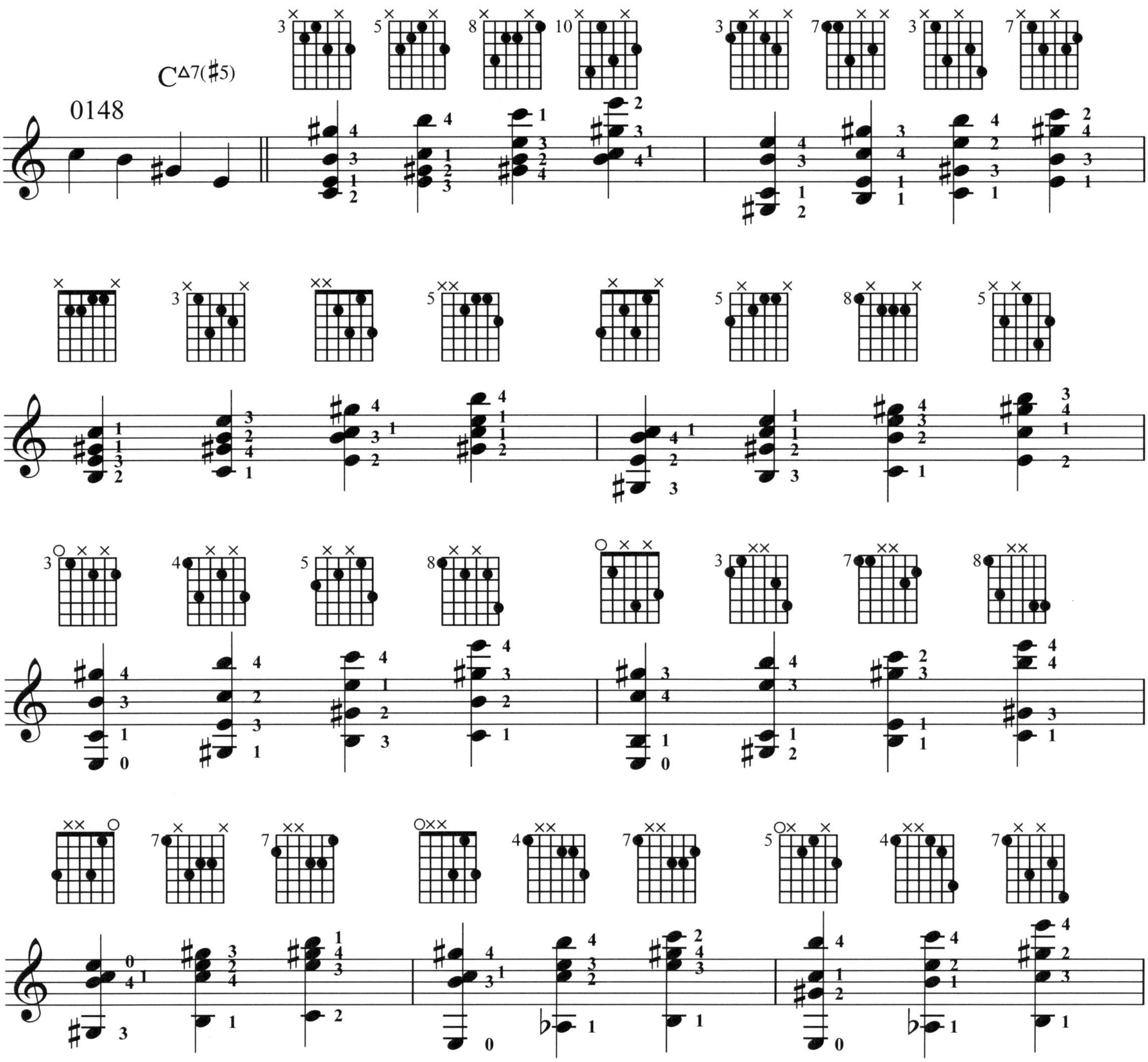

0148

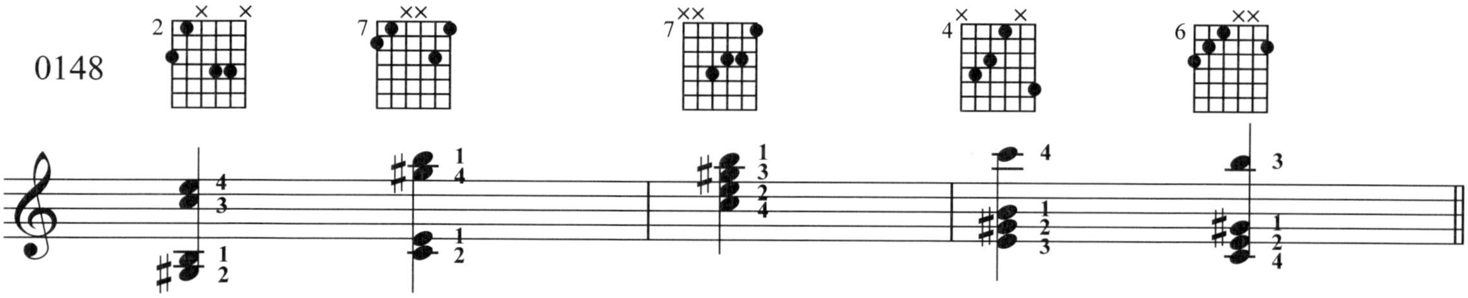

0156 Symmetrical (same as 0156, previous section)

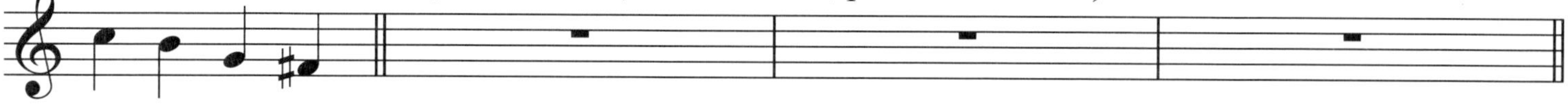

0157

$F^{(\flat 5)(9)}$

G^7sus

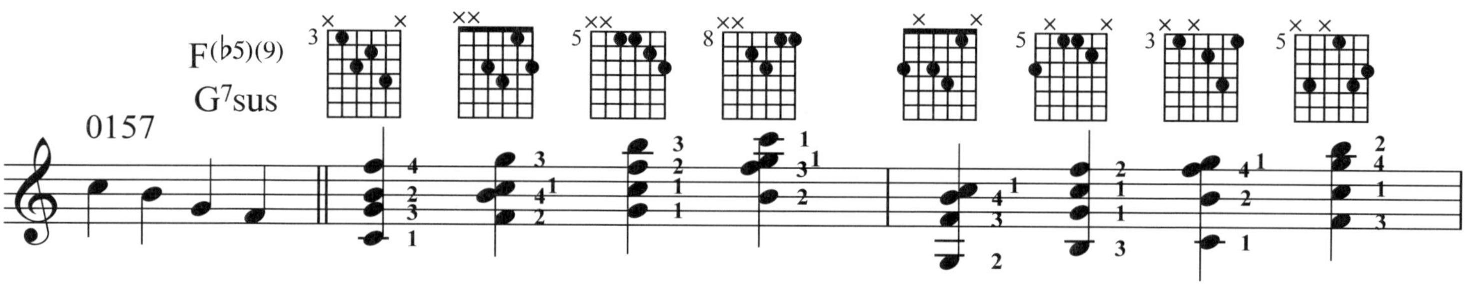

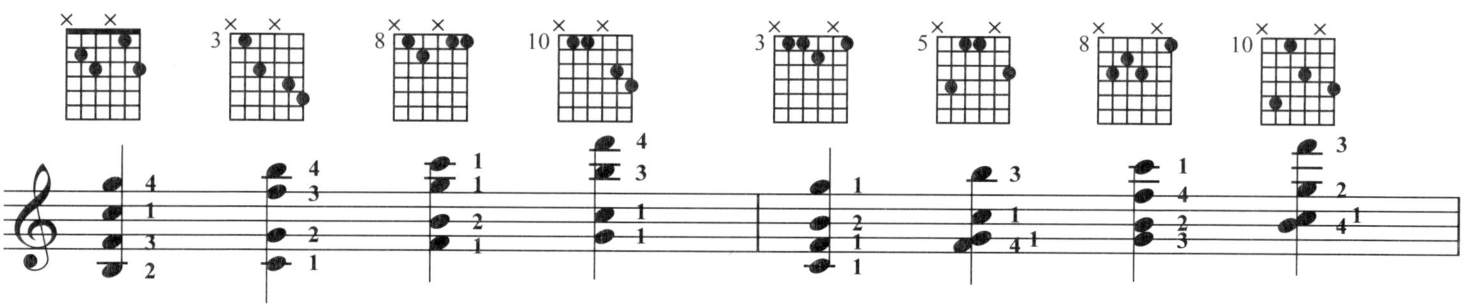

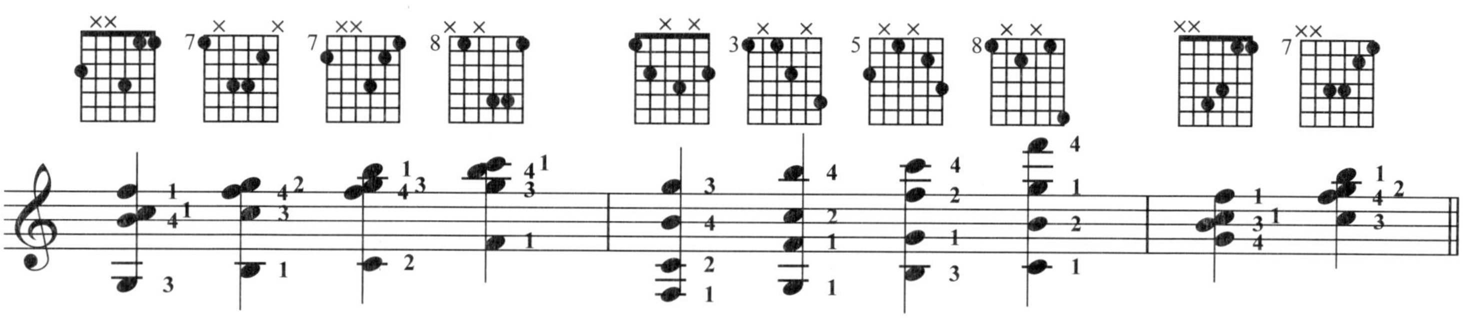

0158 Symmetrical (same as 0158, previous section)

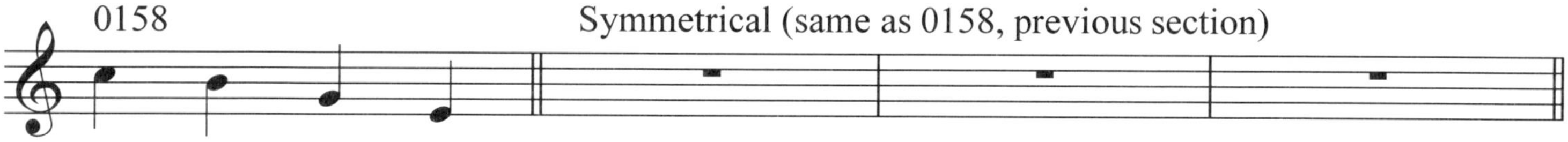

0167 Symmetrical (same as 0167, previous section)

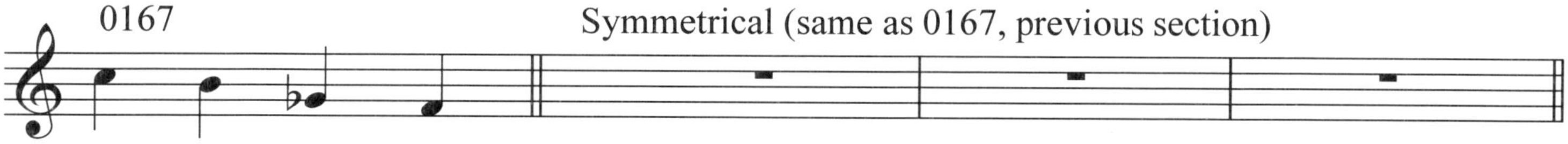

0235 Symmetrical (same as 0235, previous section)

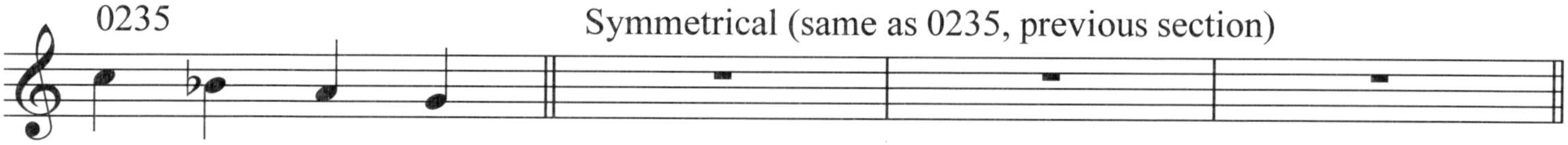

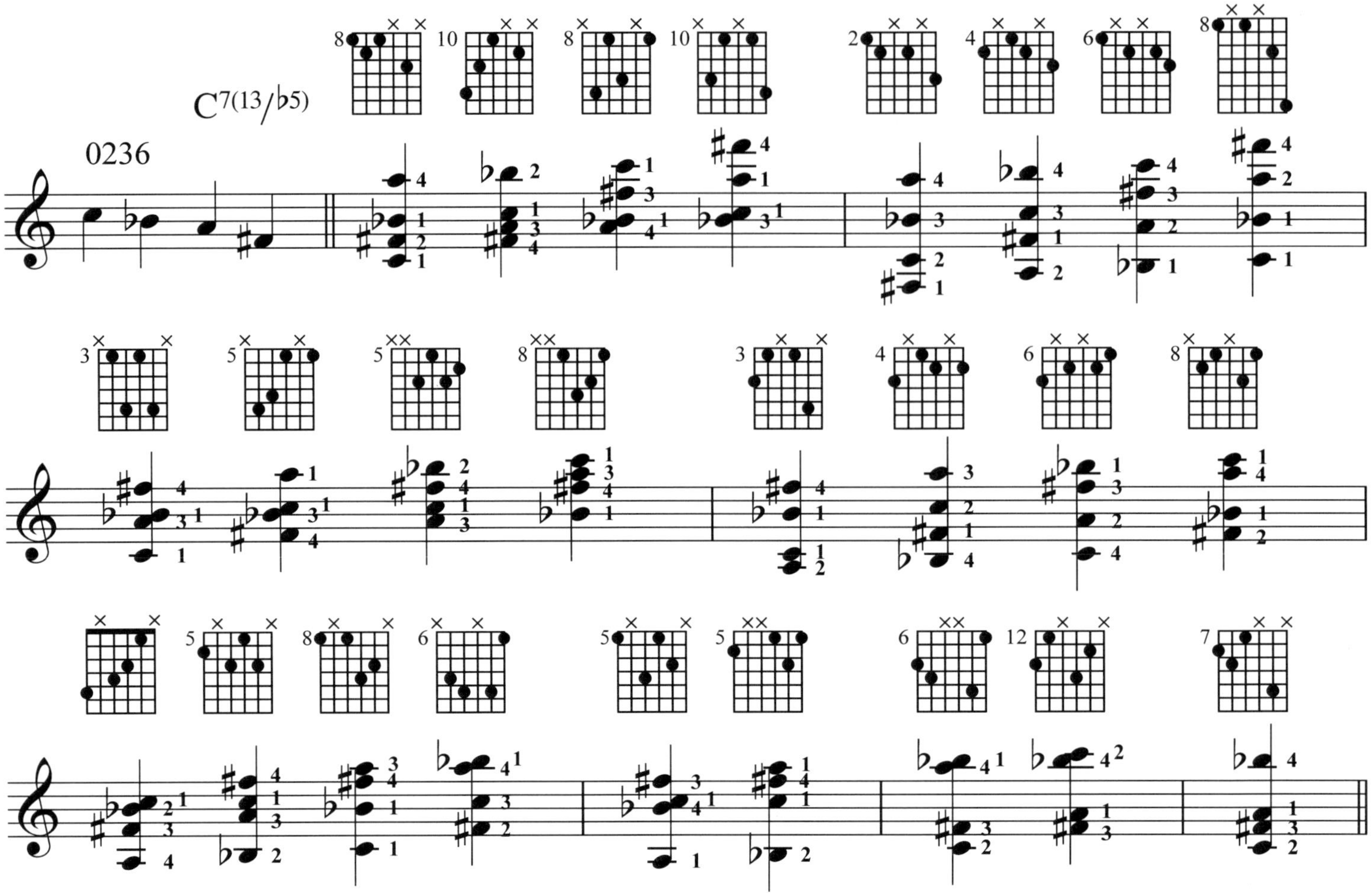
C7(13/♭5)
0236

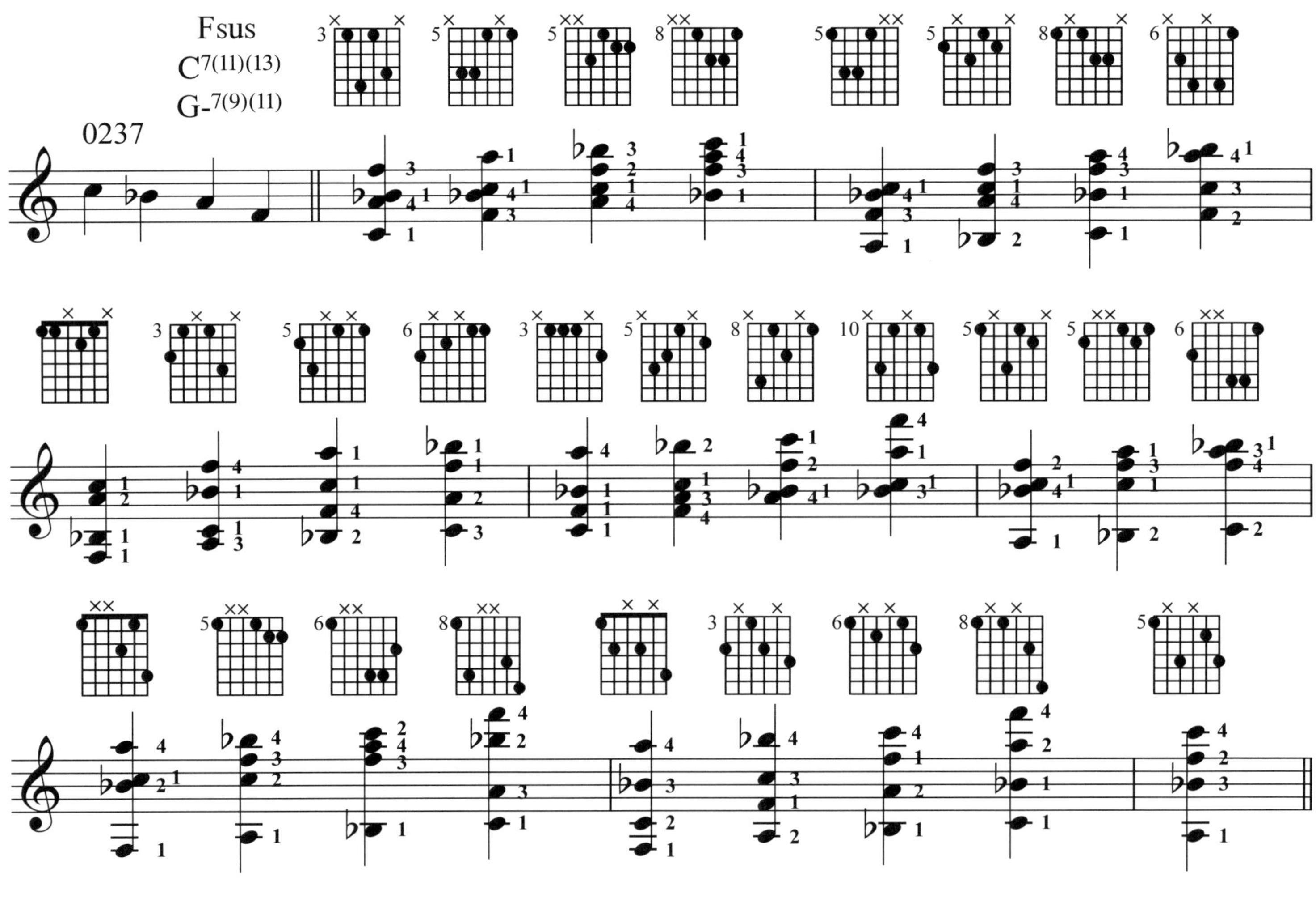
Fsus
C7(11)(13)
G-7(9)(11)
0237

0246

Symmetrical (same as 0246, previous section)

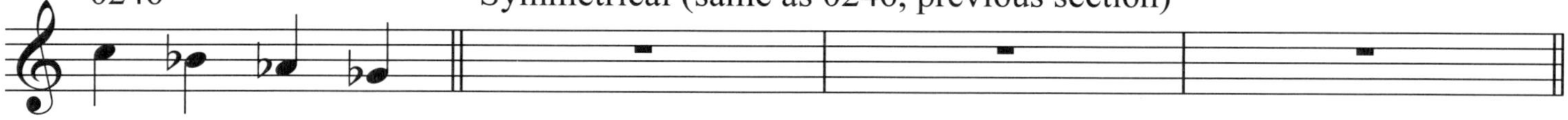

0247

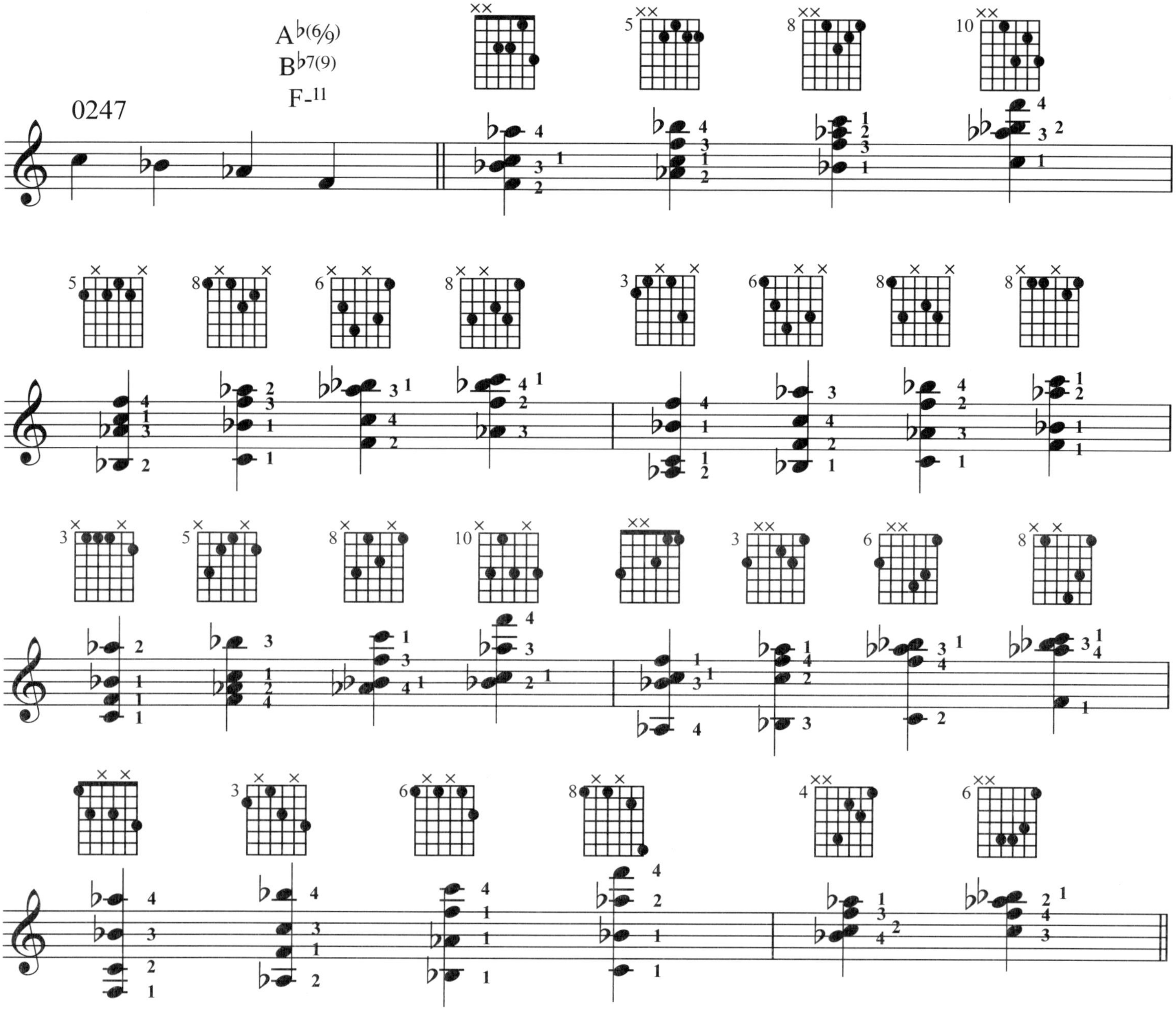

0248

Symmetrical (same as 0248, previous section)

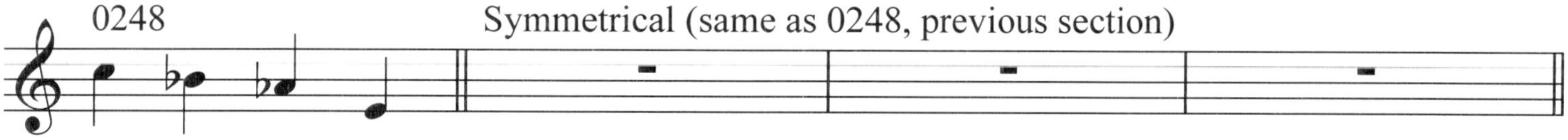

0257

Symmetrical (same as 0257, previous section)

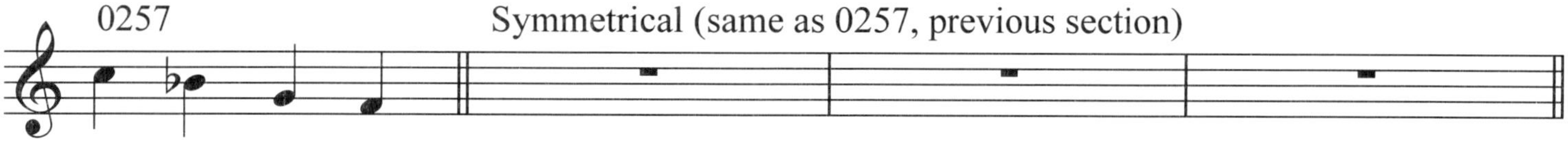

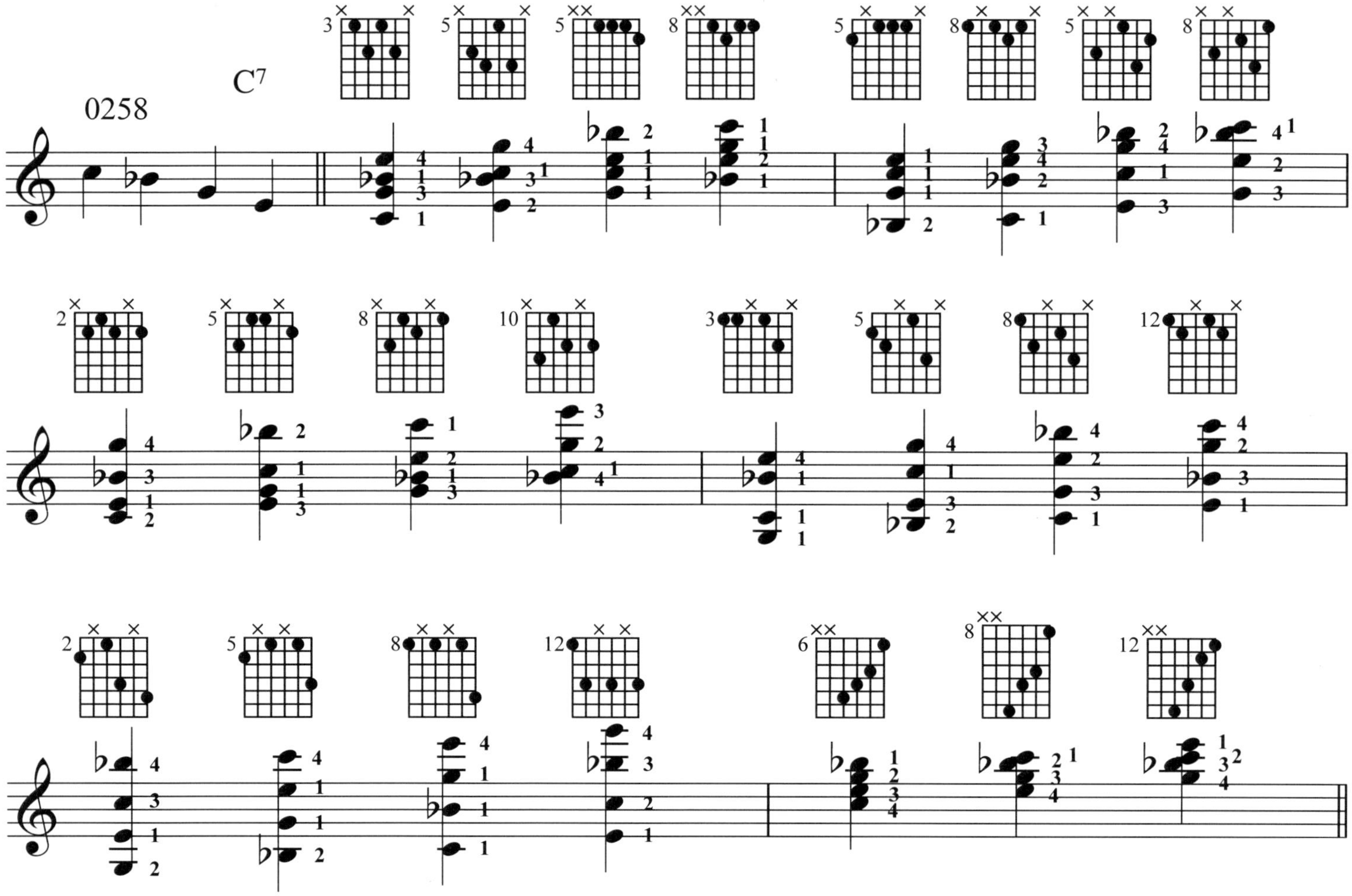

0268 Symmetrical (same as 0268, previous section)

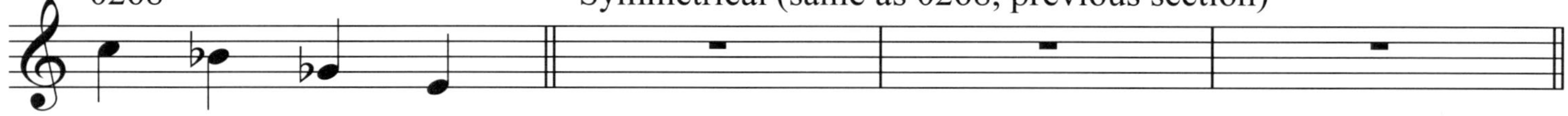

0347 Symmetrical (same as 0347, previous section)

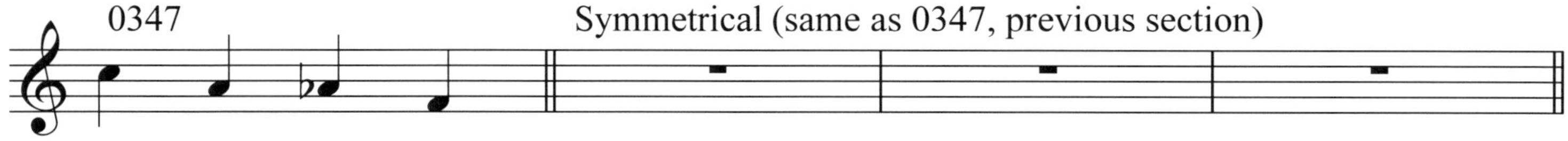

0358 Symmetrical (same as 0358, previous section)

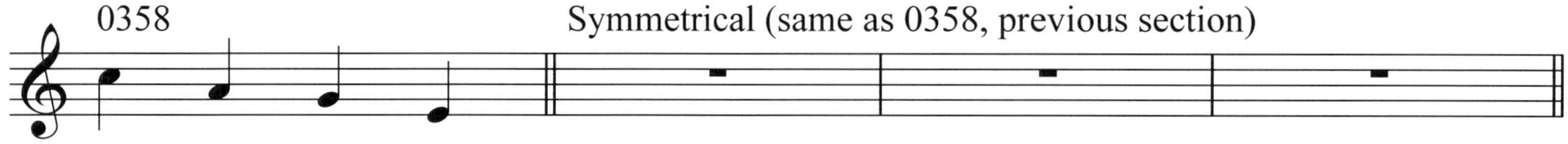

0369 Symmetrical (same as 0369, previous section)

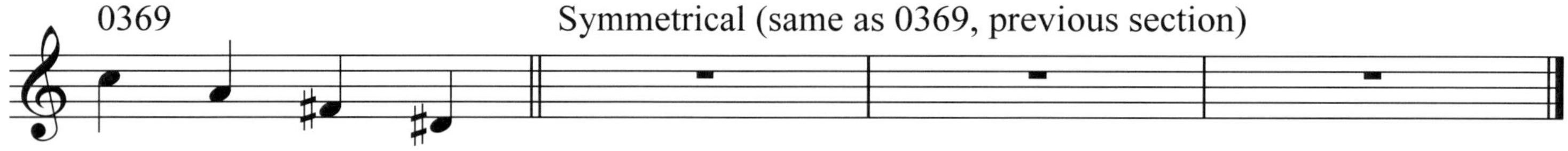

Penta-Chords

Penta-Chords

01247
F♯7(♭5/♯5)
01248
01256
01257
D♭Δ7(♭5/♭9)
01258

01267
01268
F♯7(13/♯11)
C♯-Δ7(9/11)
C(♭9/♯9/♭5)
01346

01347
E♭7(♭9/13)
01348
D♭-Δ(9)
01356
E♭-7(9/13)

01356

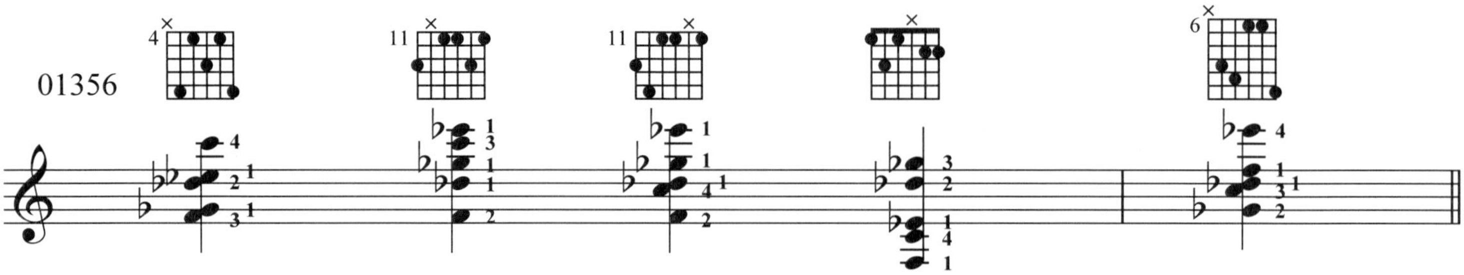

01357

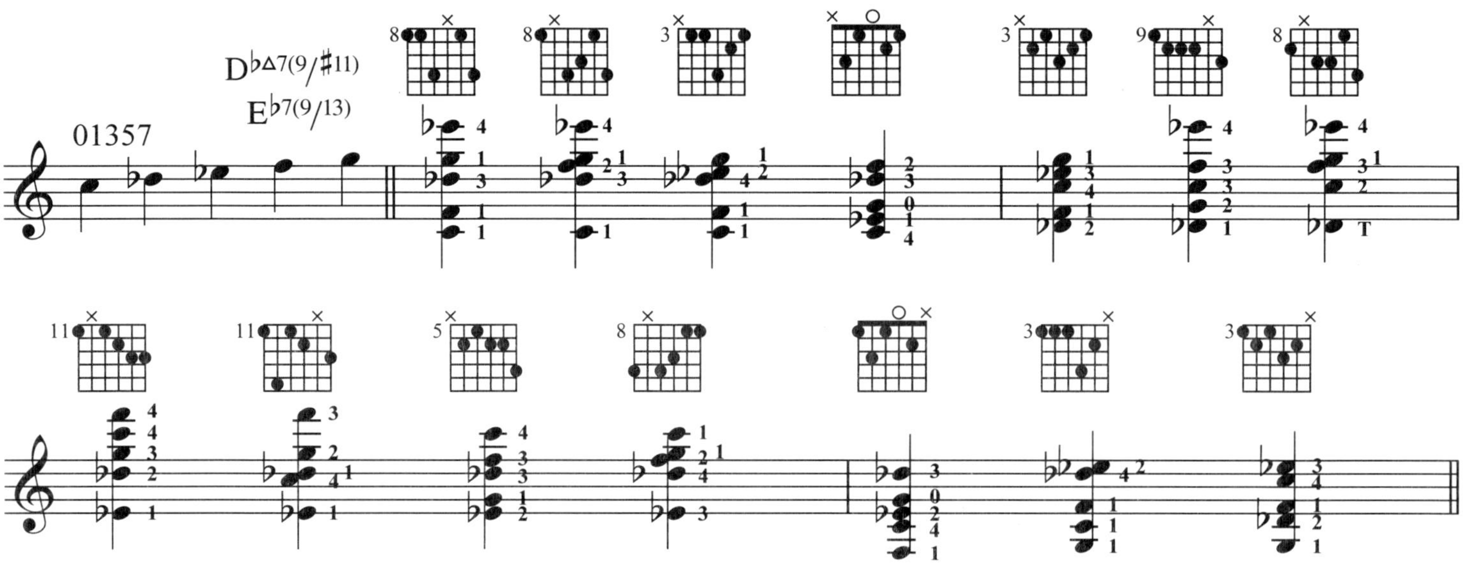

01358

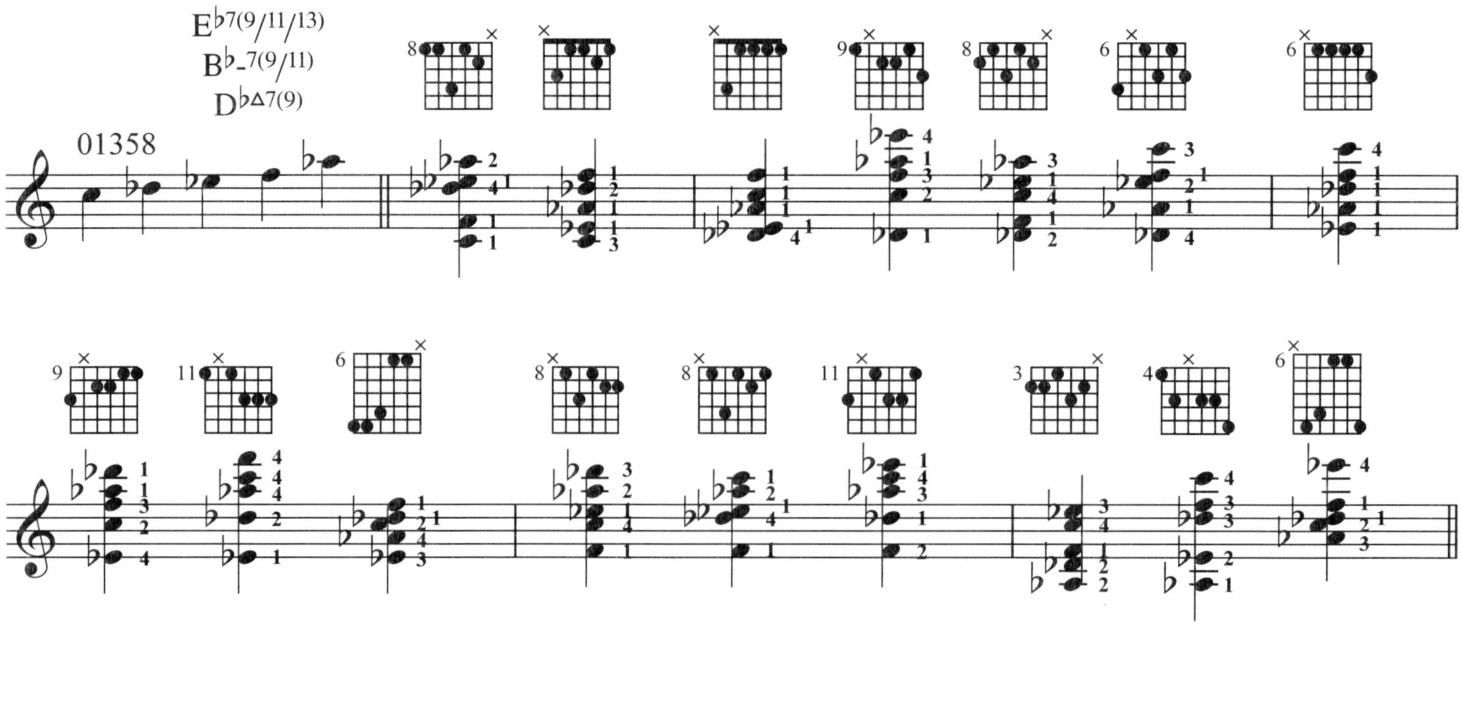

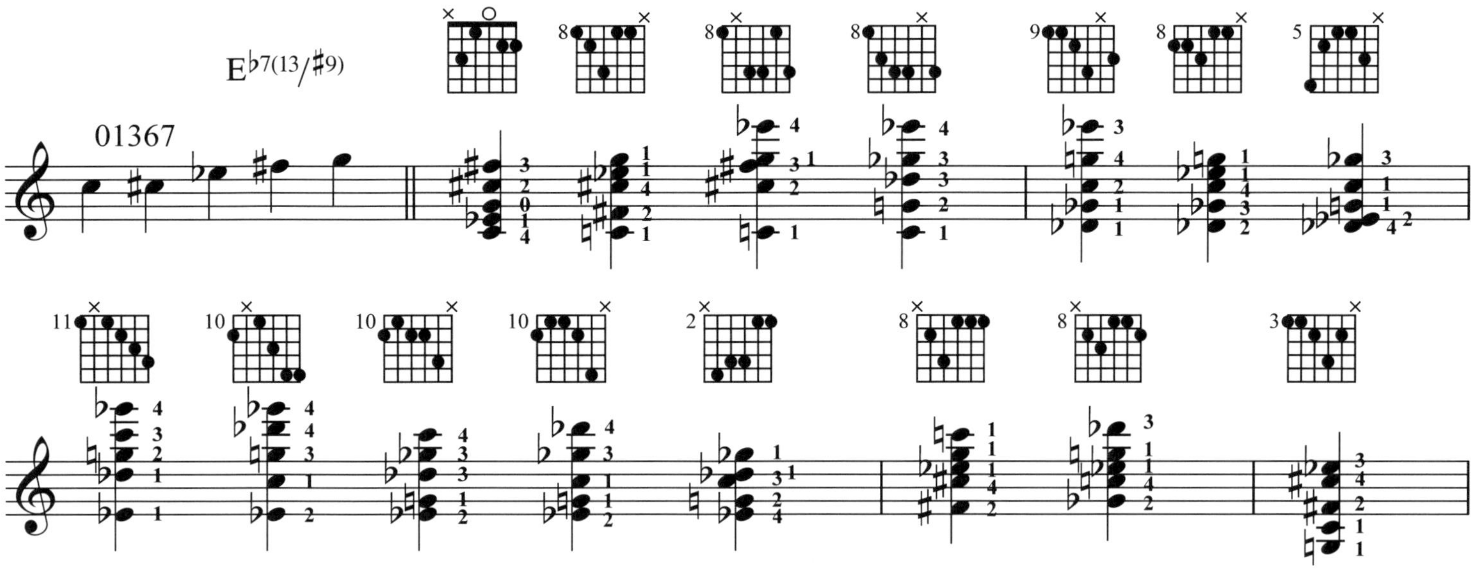
E♭7(13/♯9)
01367

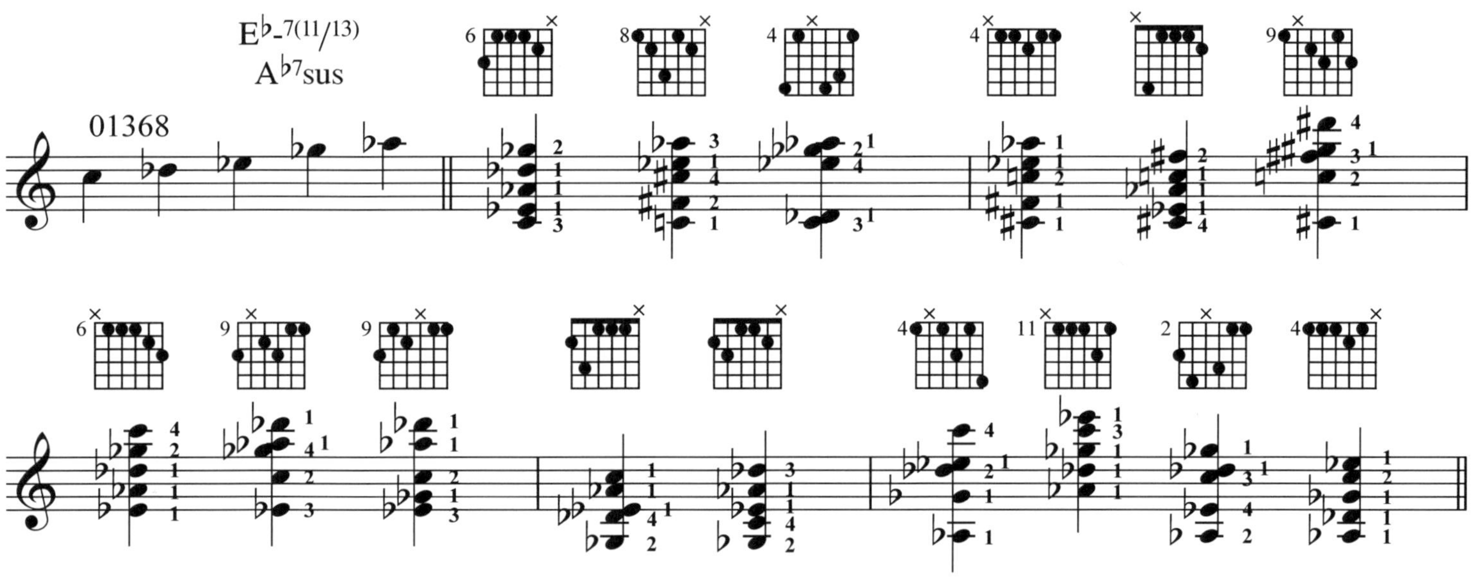
E♭-7(11/13)
A♭7sus
01368

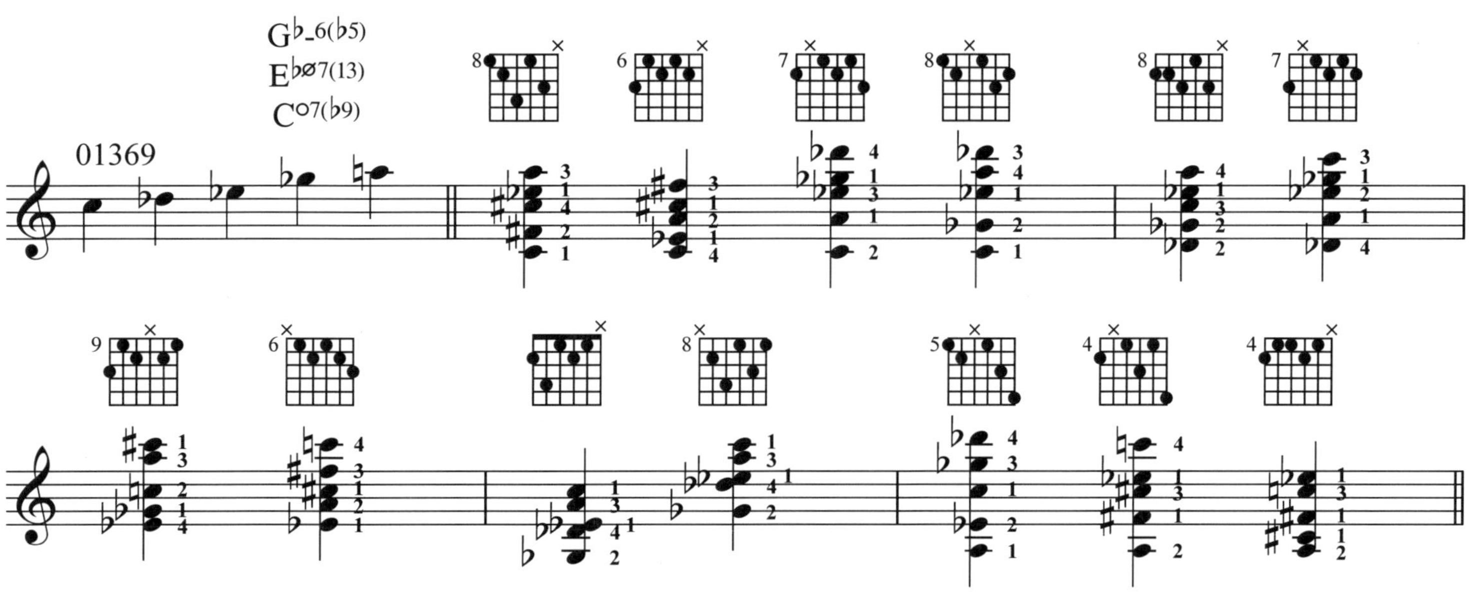
G♭-6(♭5)
E♭ø7(13)
Co7(♭9)
01369

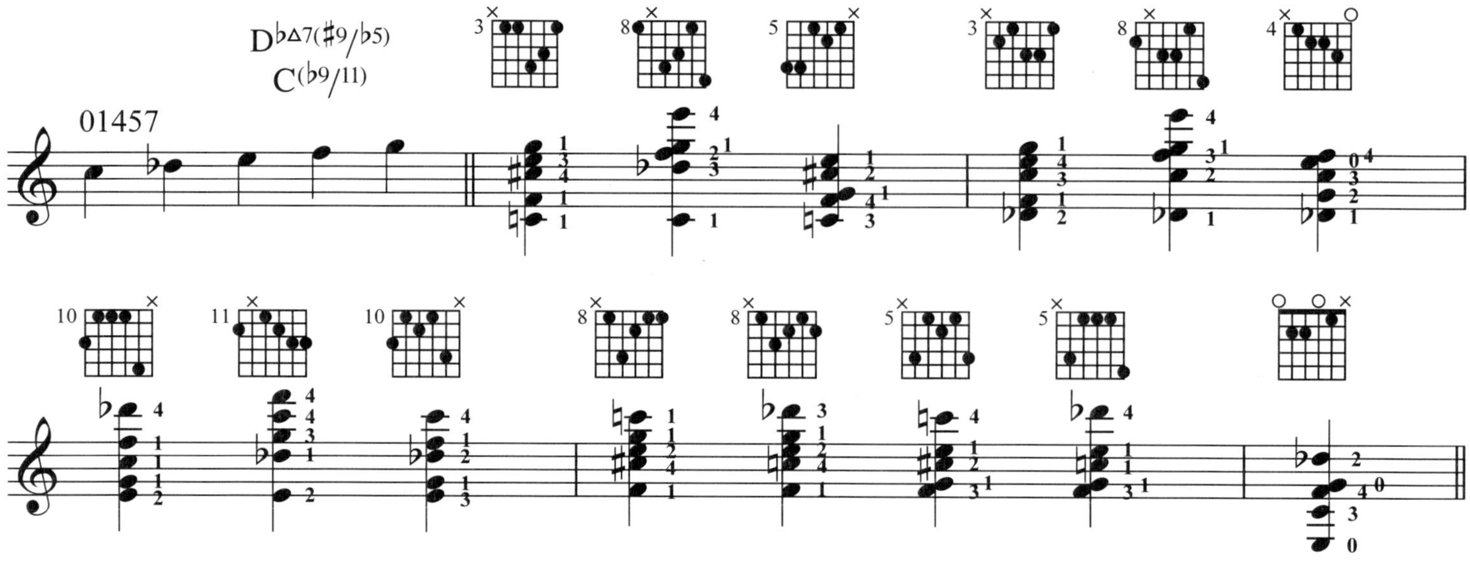
D♭Δ7(♯9/♭5)
C(♭9/11)
01457

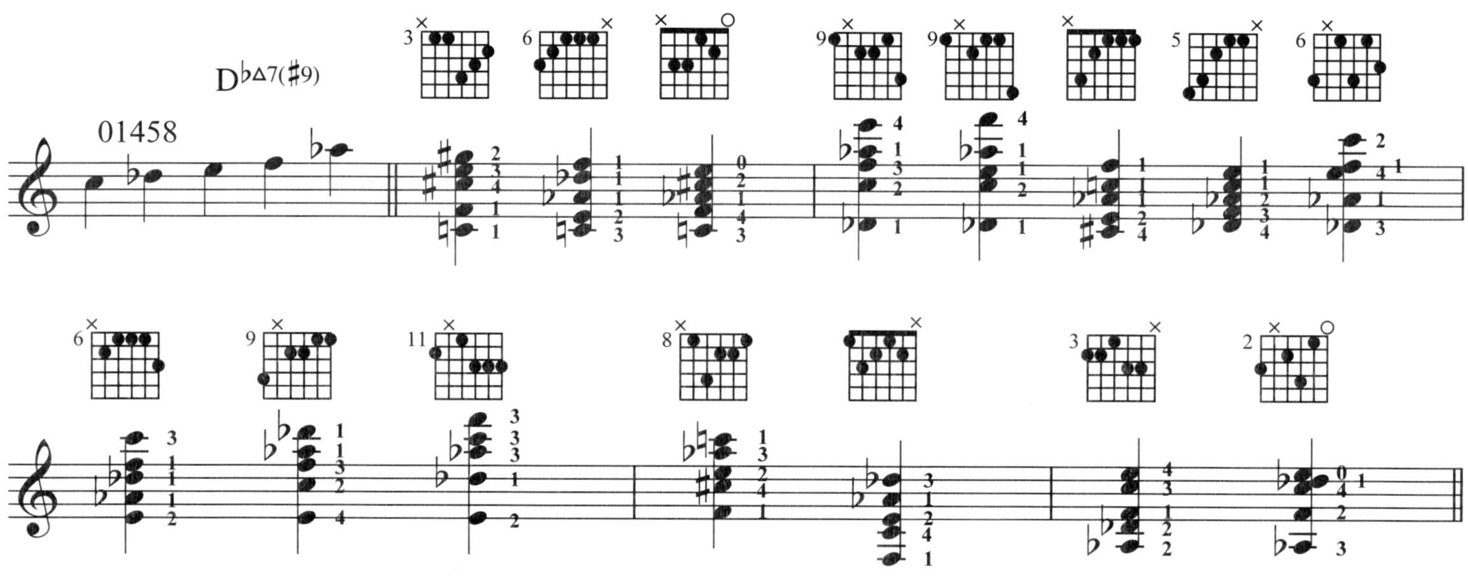
D♭Δ7(♯9)
01458

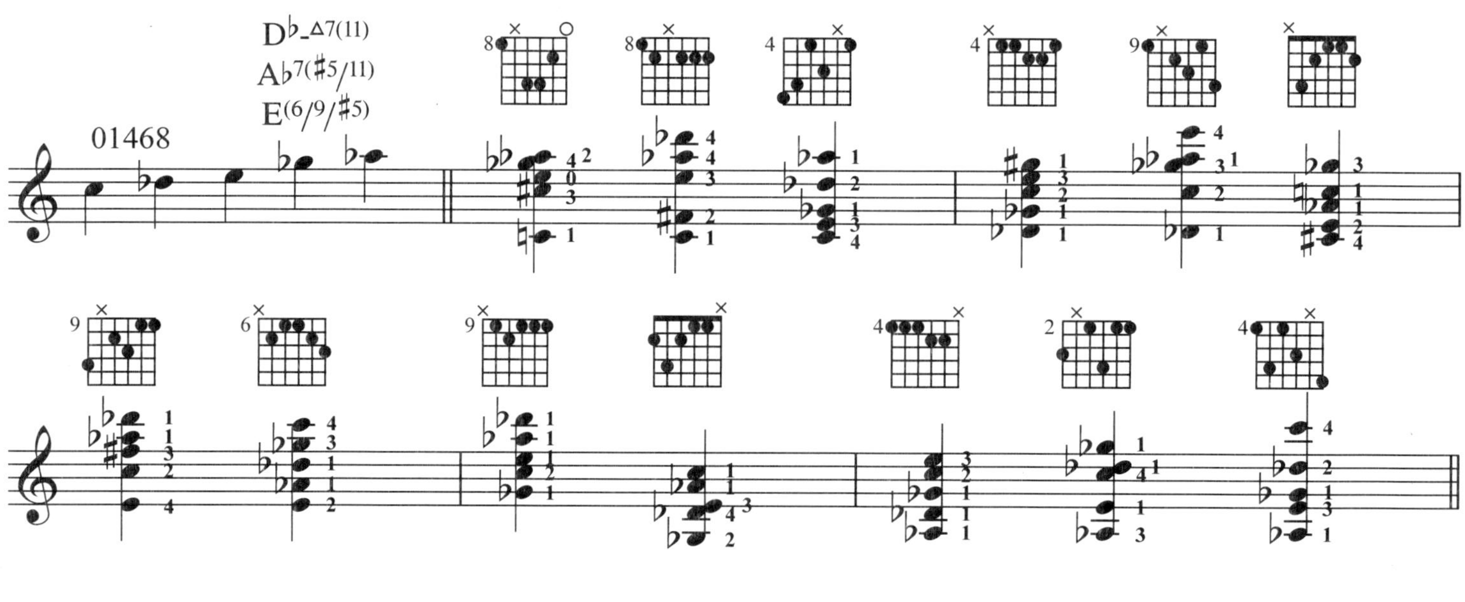
D♭-Δ7(11)
A♭7(♯5/11)
E(6/9/♯5)
01468

C6(♭5/♭9)
A6(♯9)
01469
E6(♯9/♯5)
C(♯5/♭9)
C♯-Δ7(♭5)
01478
A♭7(sus13)
G♭Δ7(9/♯11)
F-(♭9/♯5)
D♭Δ7(11)
01568

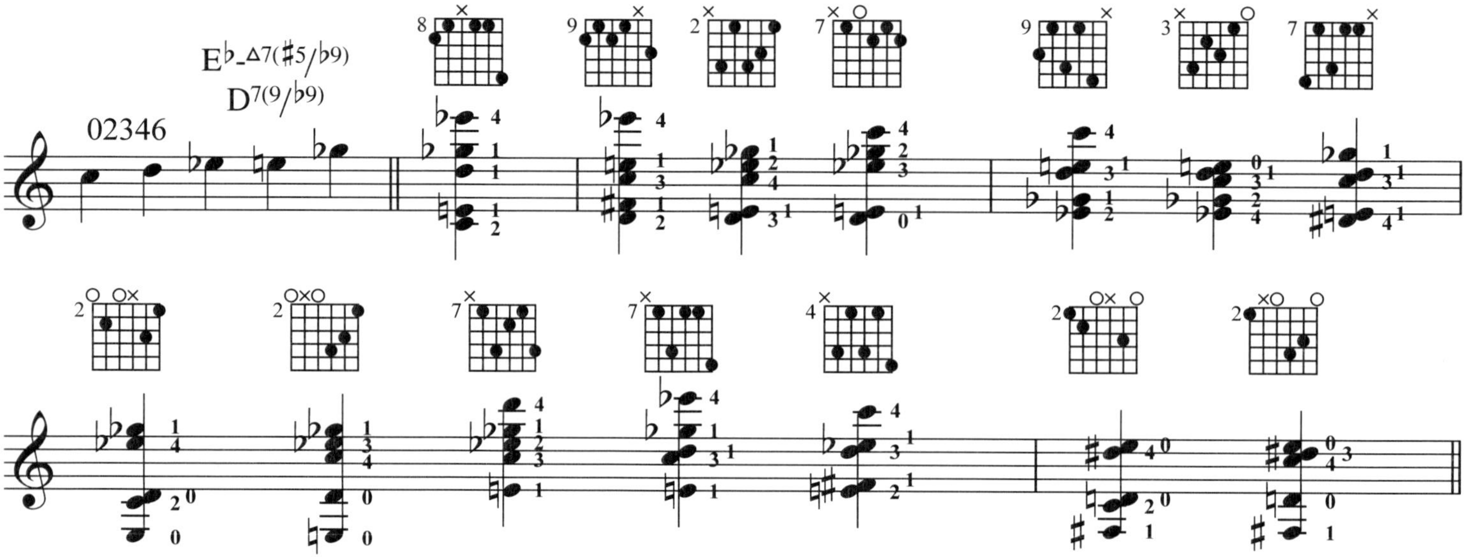
02346
E♭-Δ7(♯5/♭9)
D7(9/♭9)

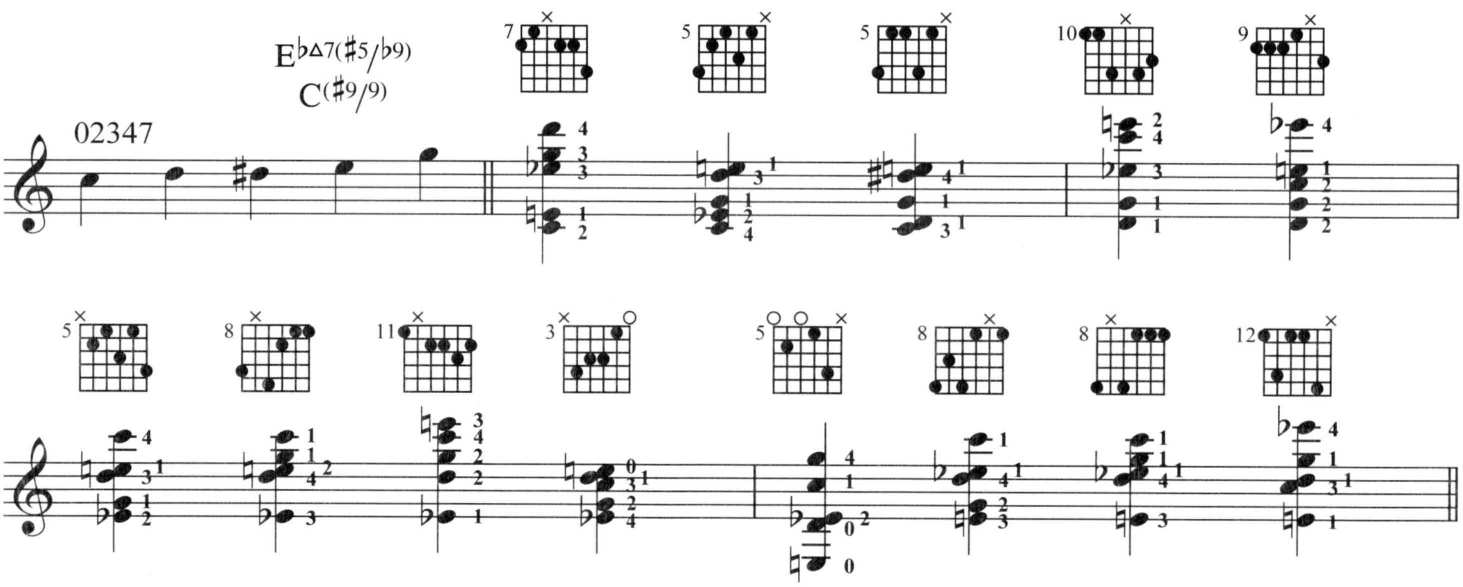
02347
E♭Δ7(♯5/♭9)
C(♯9/9)

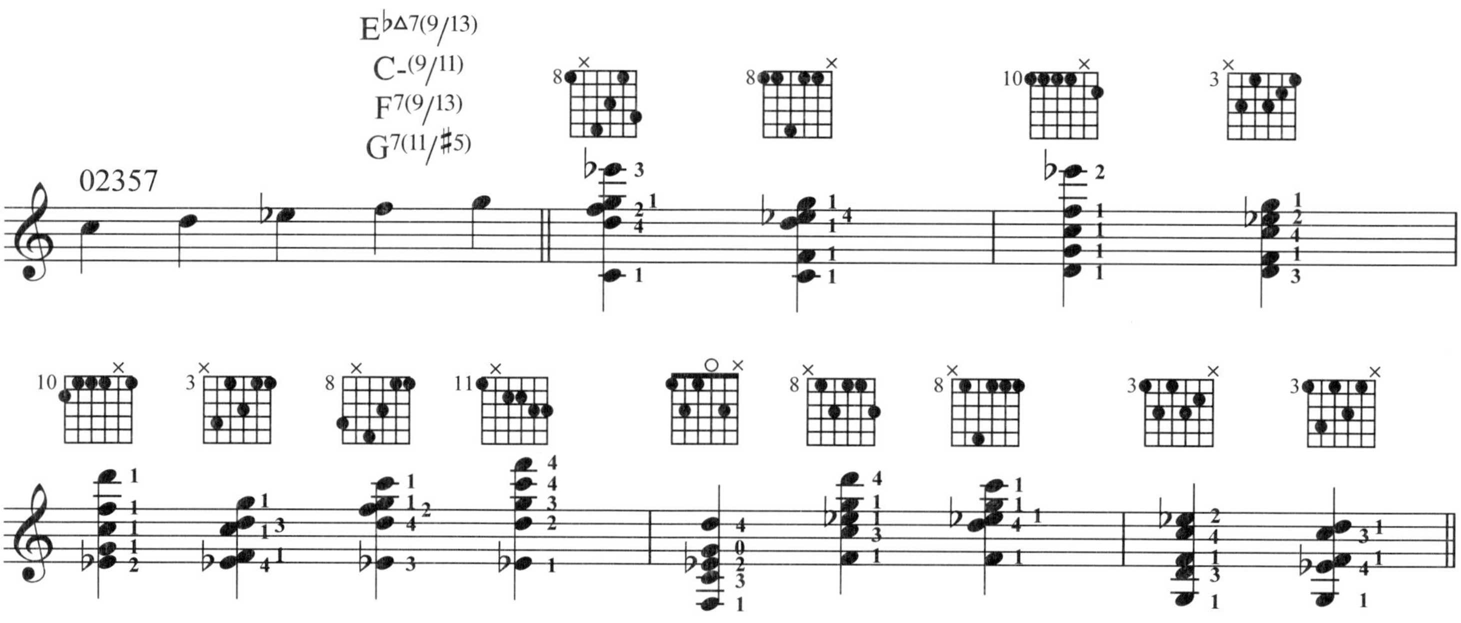
02357
E♭Δ7(9/13)
C-(9/11)
F7(9/13)
G7(11/♯5)

A♭Δ7(♭5)
02358
D7(♭5/♭9)
A♭7(♭5)
02368
E7(♭9/♯5)
F-Δ7(13)
Dø7(9)
02458
D7(9/♯11))
E7(9/♯5)
02468
D/C
D7(9)
02469

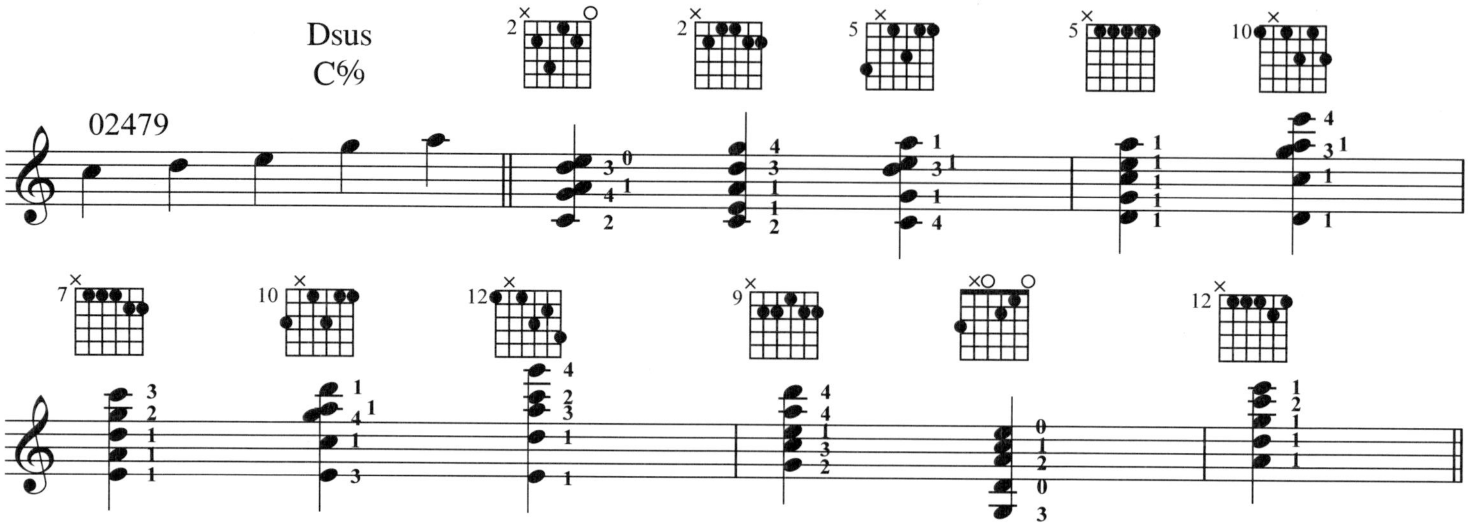
Dsus
C6/9
02479

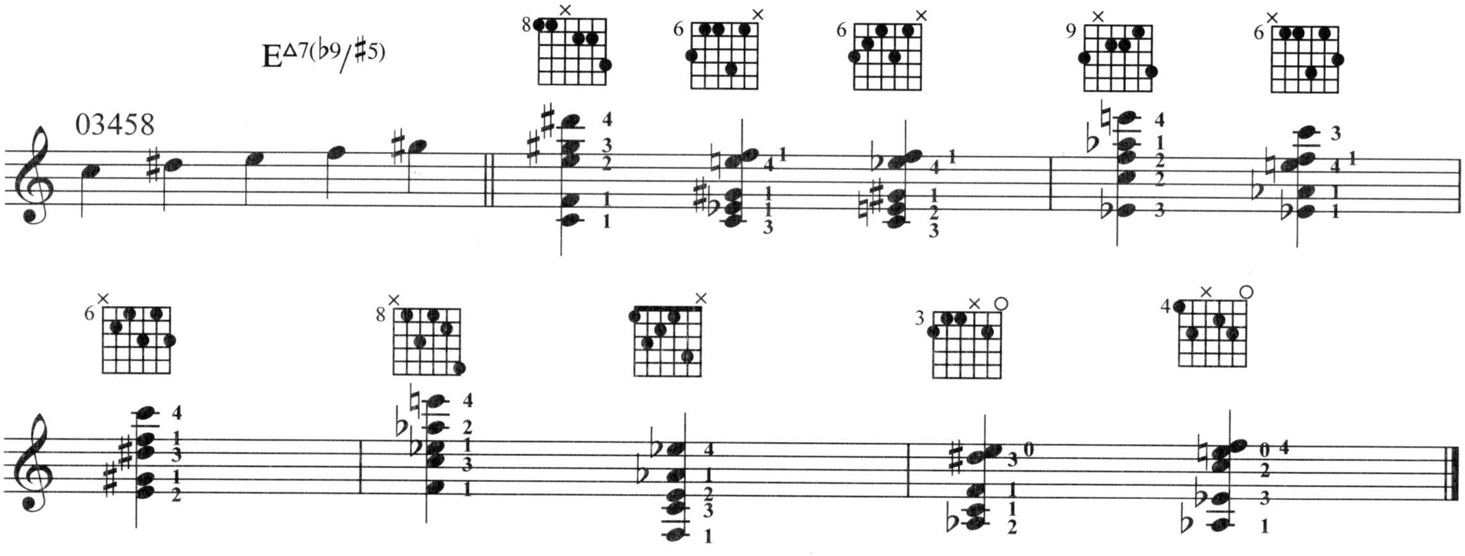
EΔ7(♭9/♯5)
03458

Inverted Penta-Chords

Inverted Penta-Chords

01246

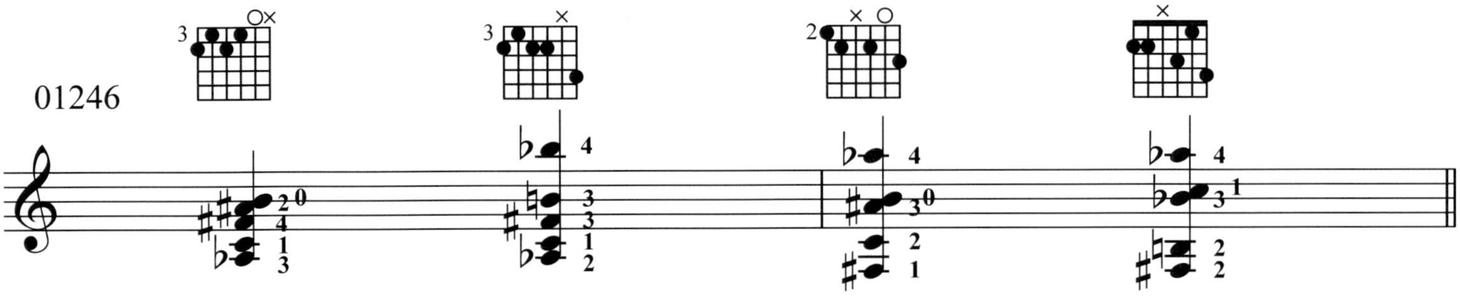

01247

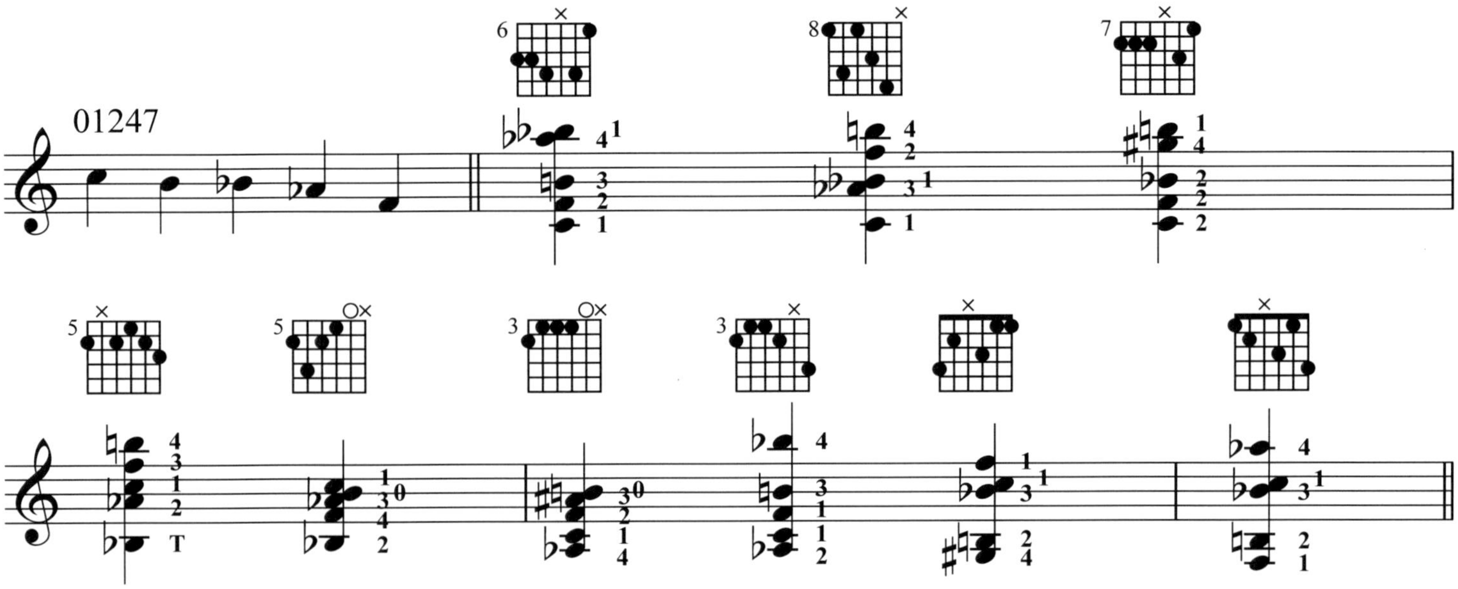

01248

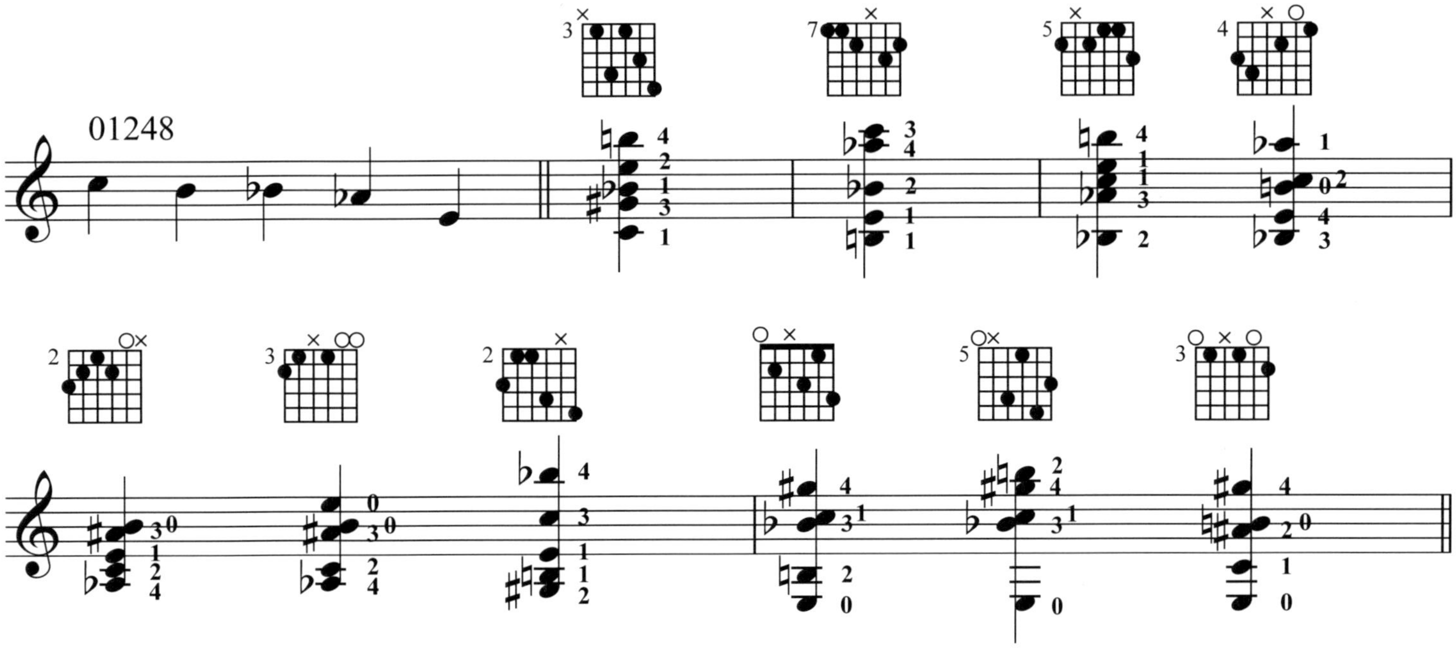

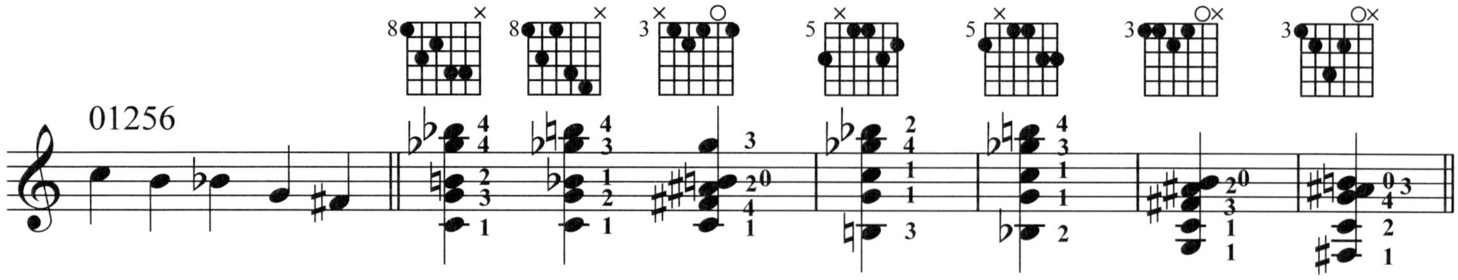
01256

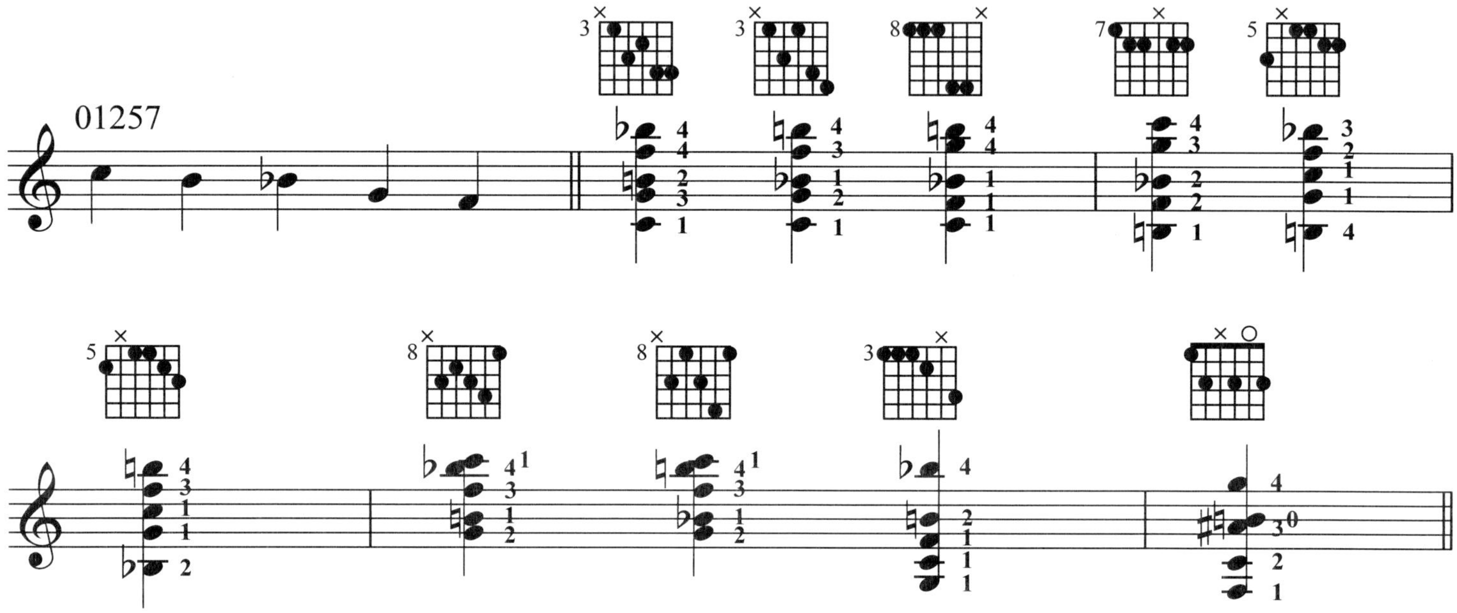
01257

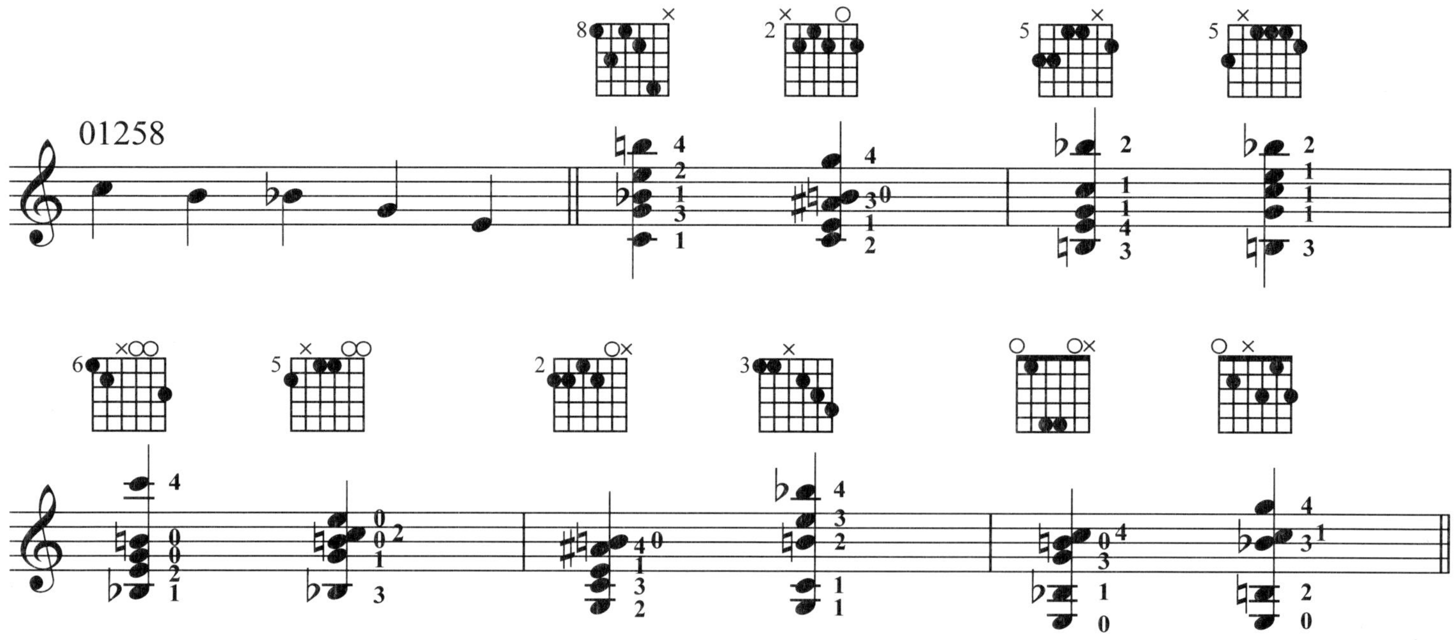
01258

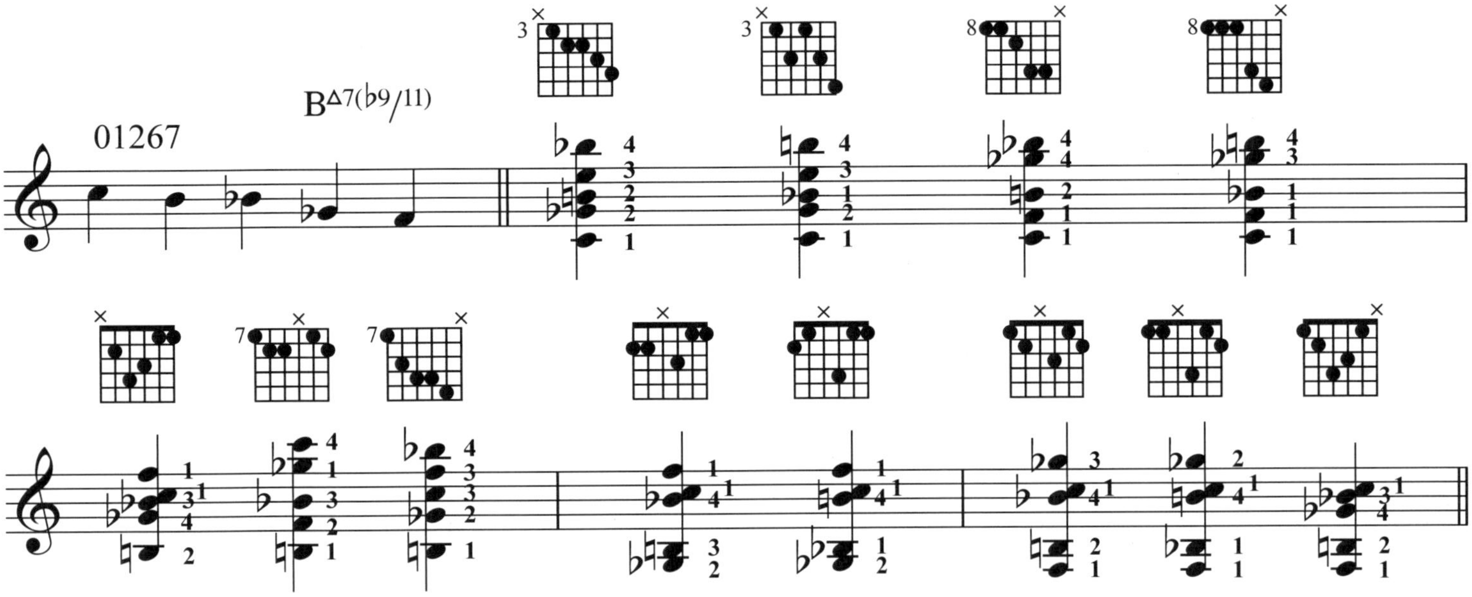
B△7(♭9/11)
01267

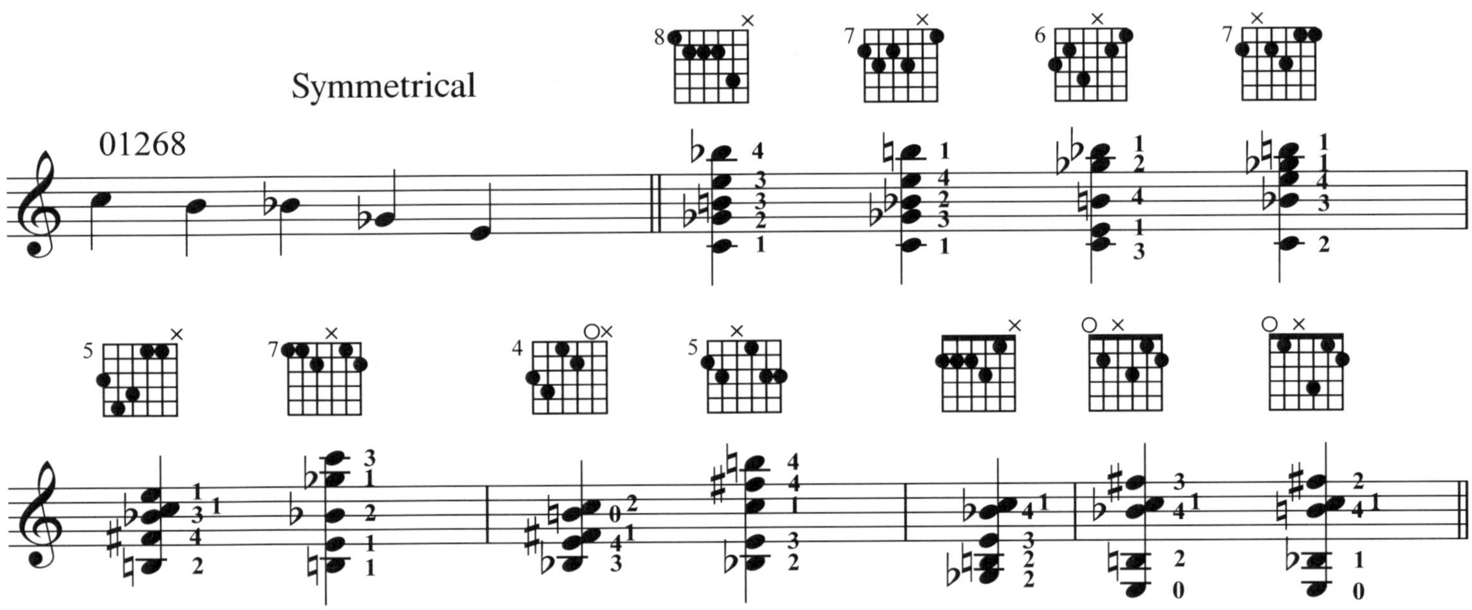
Symmetrical
01268

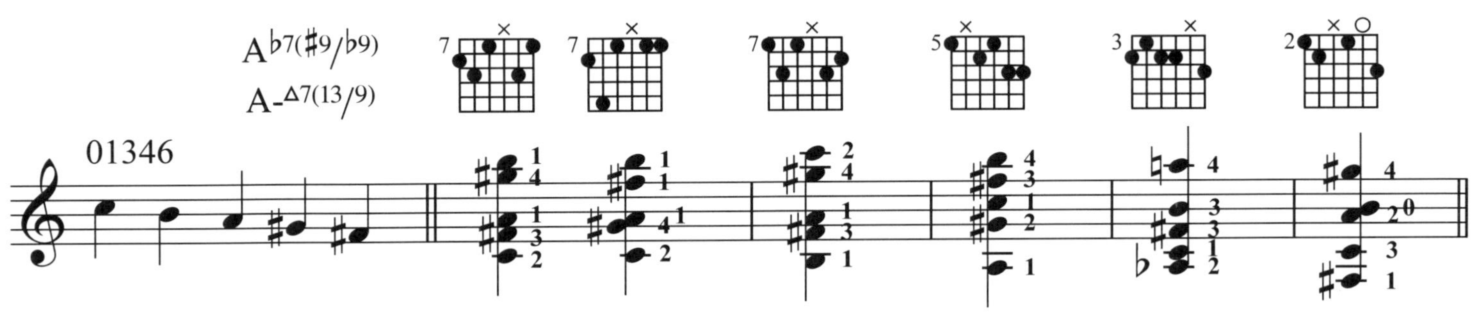
A♭7(♯9/♭9)
A-△7(13/9)
01346

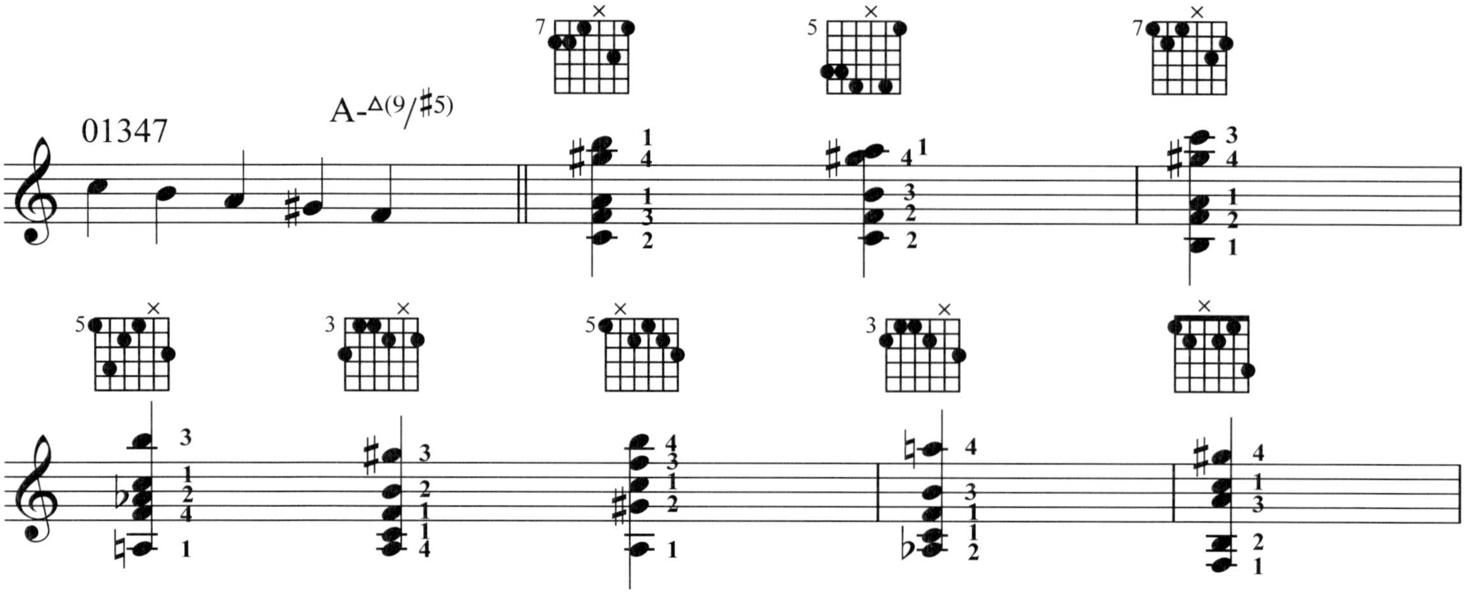
01347
A-Δ(9/♯5)

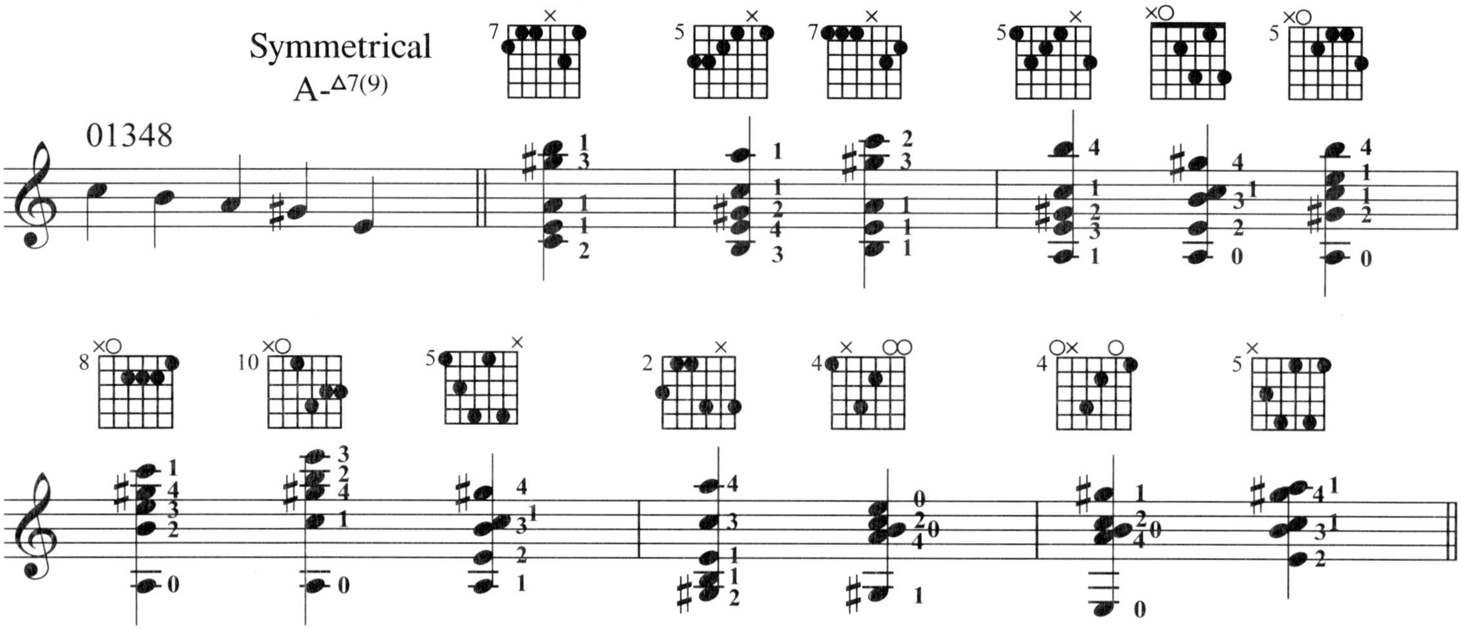
Symmetrical
A-Δ7(9)
01348

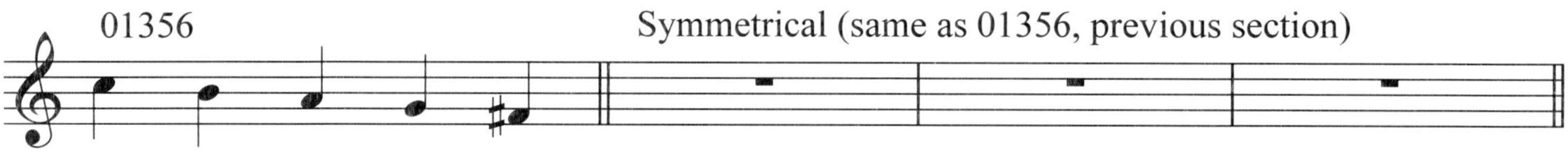
01356
Symmetrical (same as 01356, previous section)

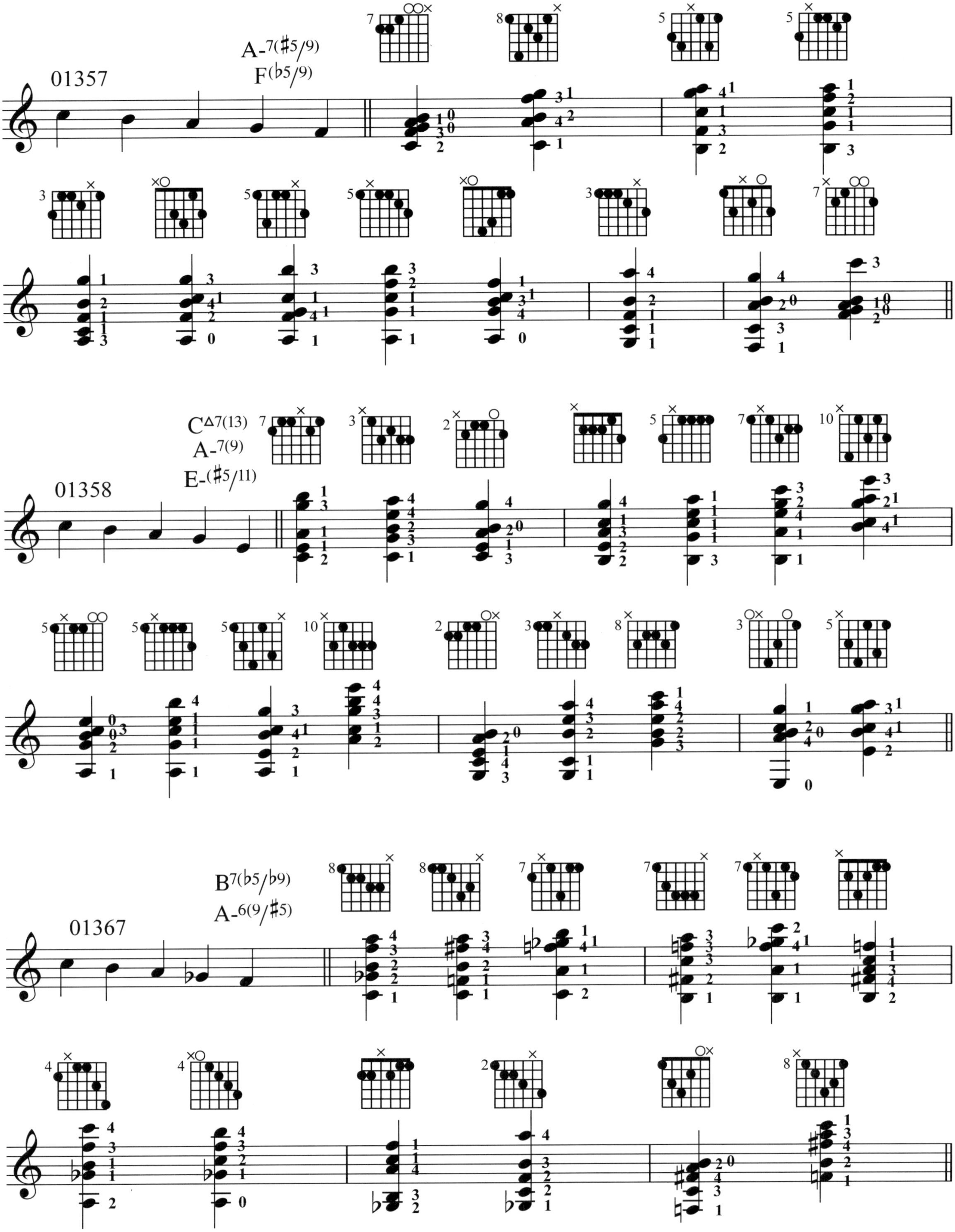
01357
A-7(♯5/9)
F(♭5/9)
01358
CΔ7(13)
A-7(9)
E-(♯5/11)
01367
B7(♭5/♭9)
A-6(9/♯5)

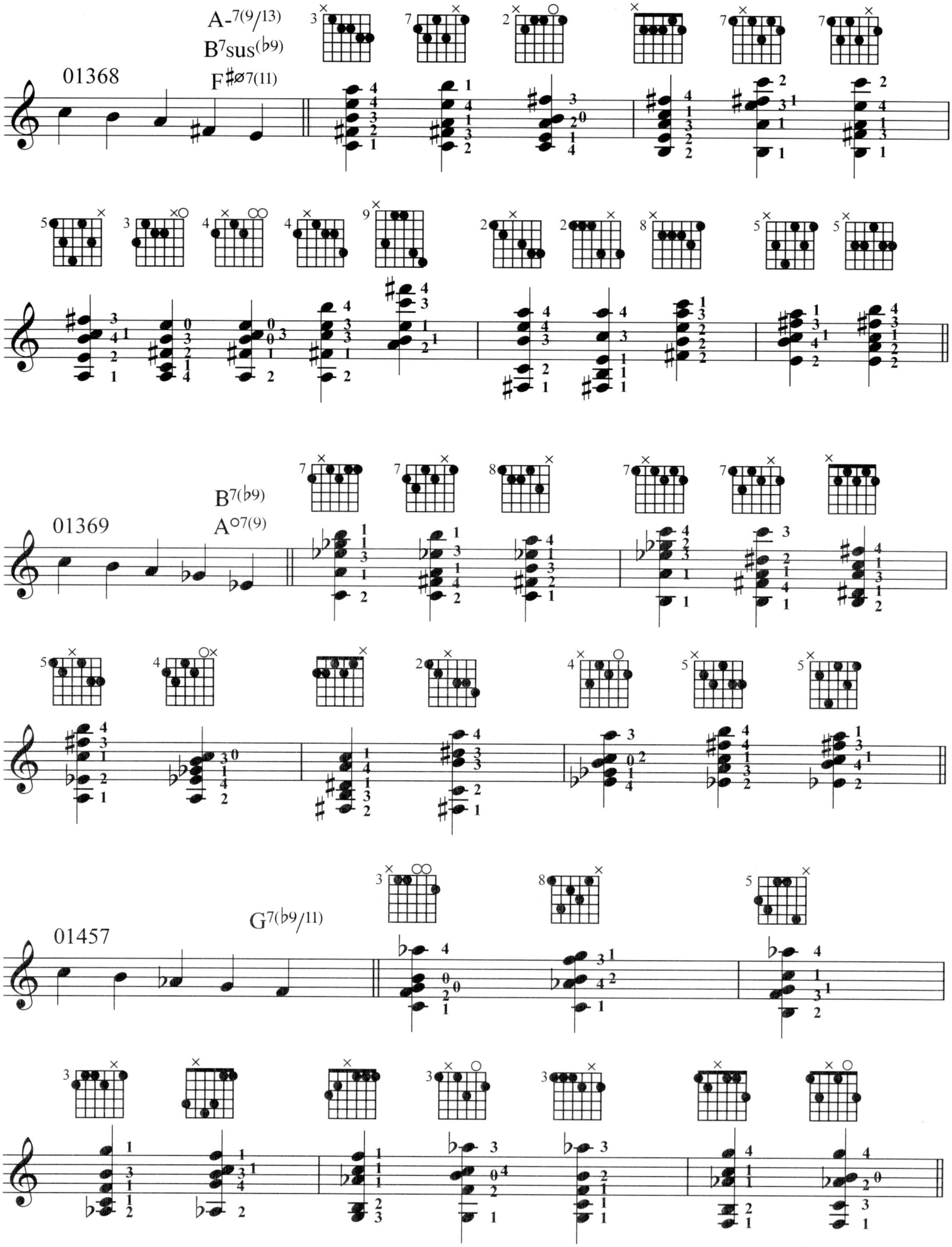
01368
A-7(9/13)
B7sus(♭9)
F♯ø7(11)
01369
B7(♭9)
A°7(9)
01457
G7(♭9/11)

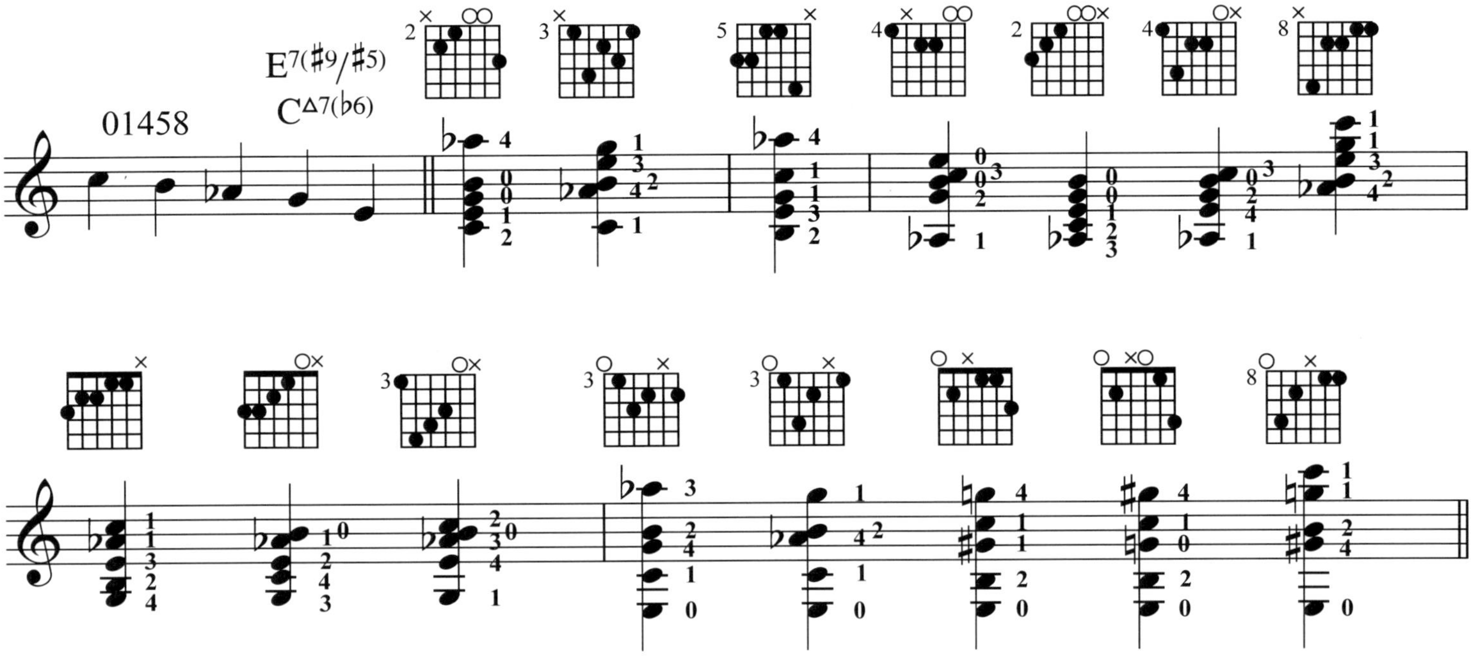
01458
E7(♯9/♯5)
C∆7(♭6)

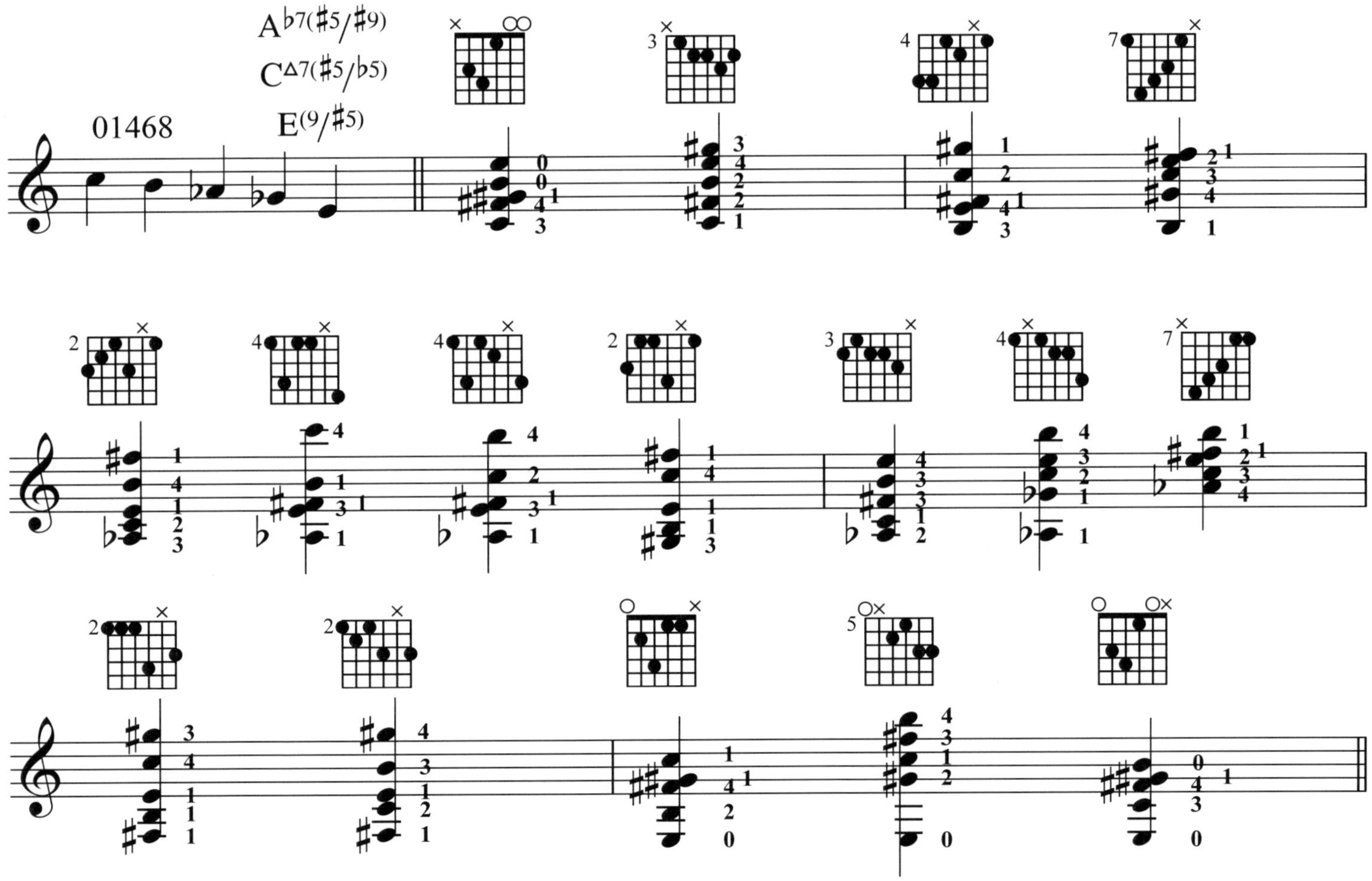
01468
A♭7(♯5/♯9)
C∆7(♯5/♭5)
E(9/♯5)

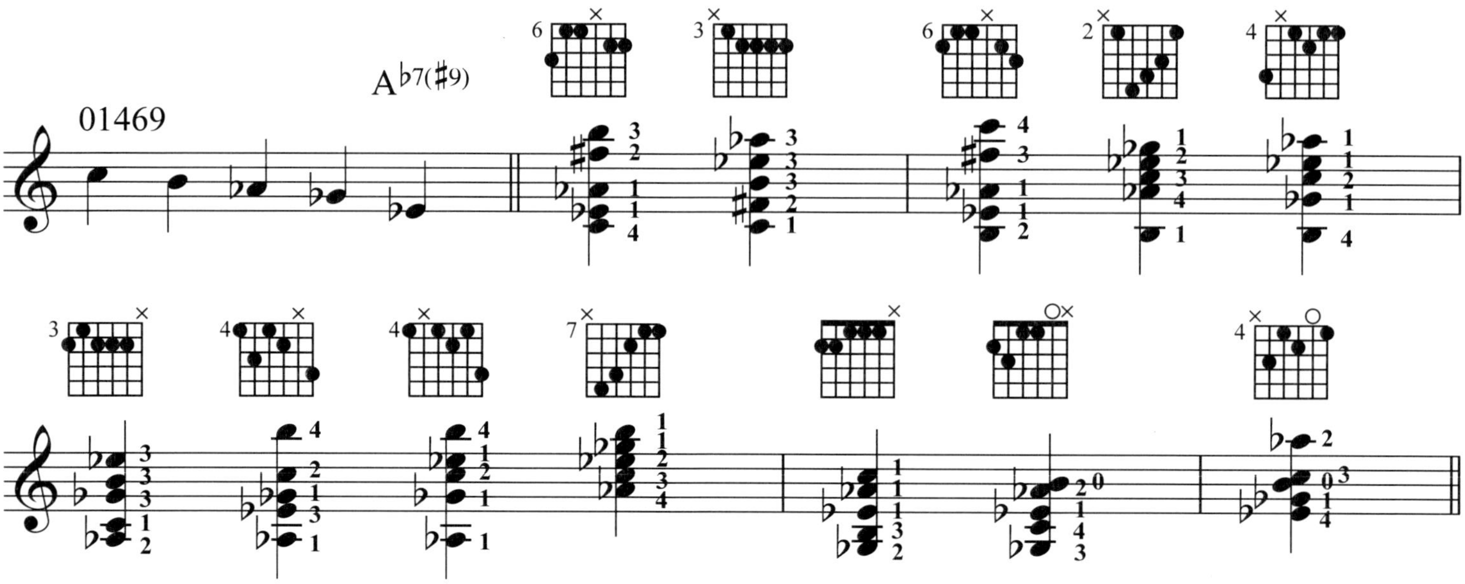
01469
A♭7(♯9)

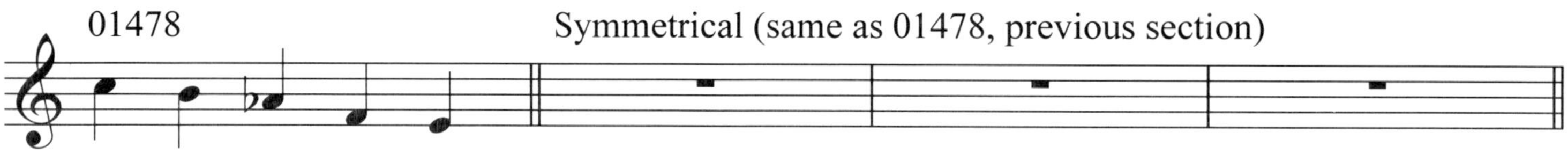
01478
Symmetrical (same as 01478, previous section)

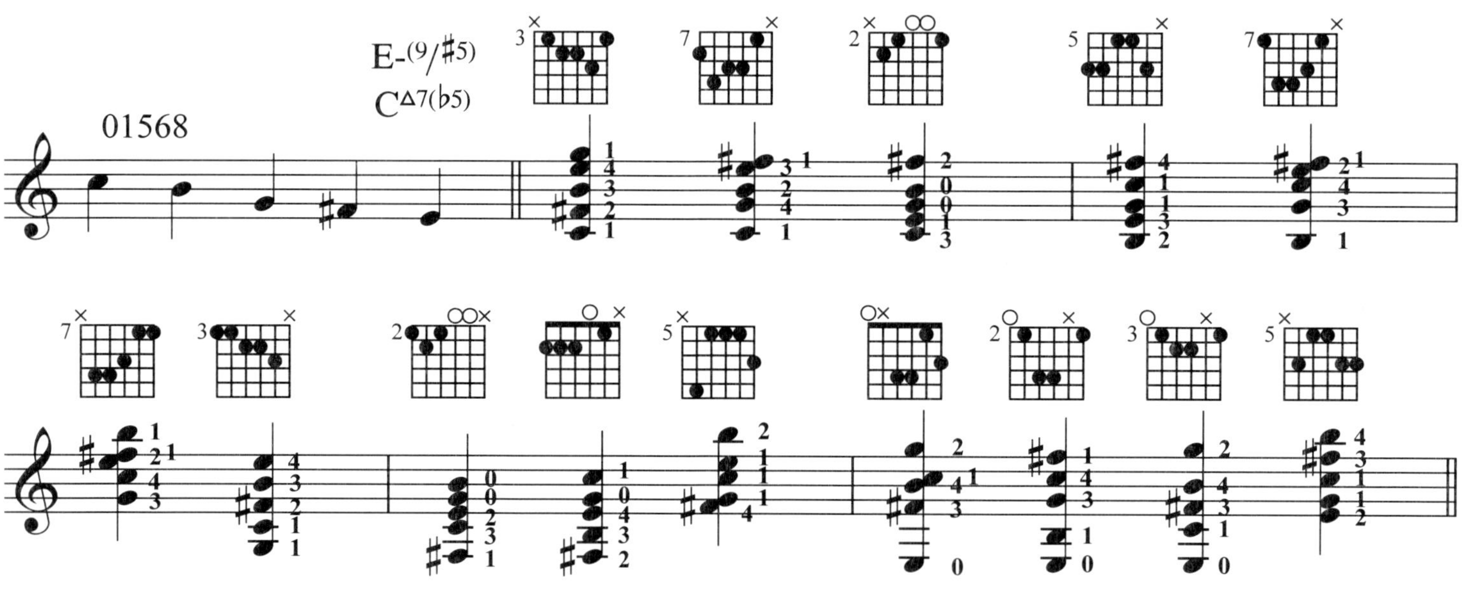
01568
E-(9/♯5)
C∆7(♭5)

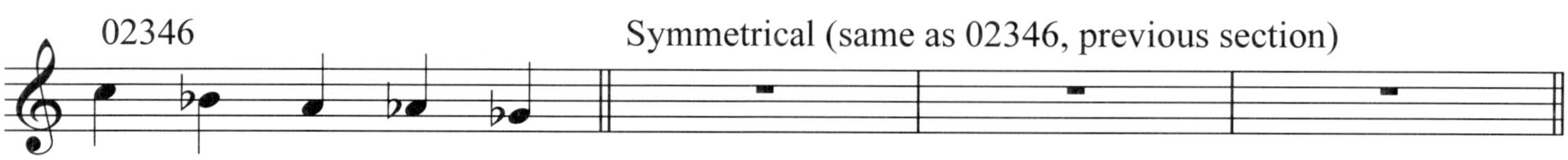
02346
Symmetrical (same as 02346, previous section)

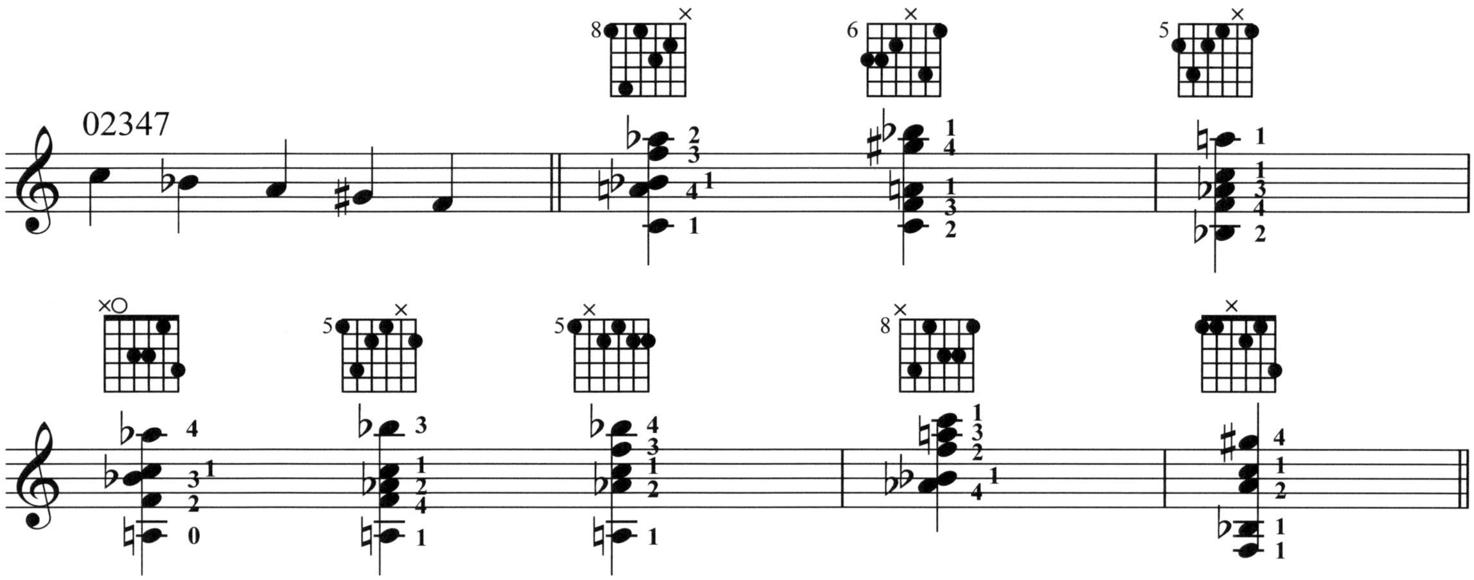
02347

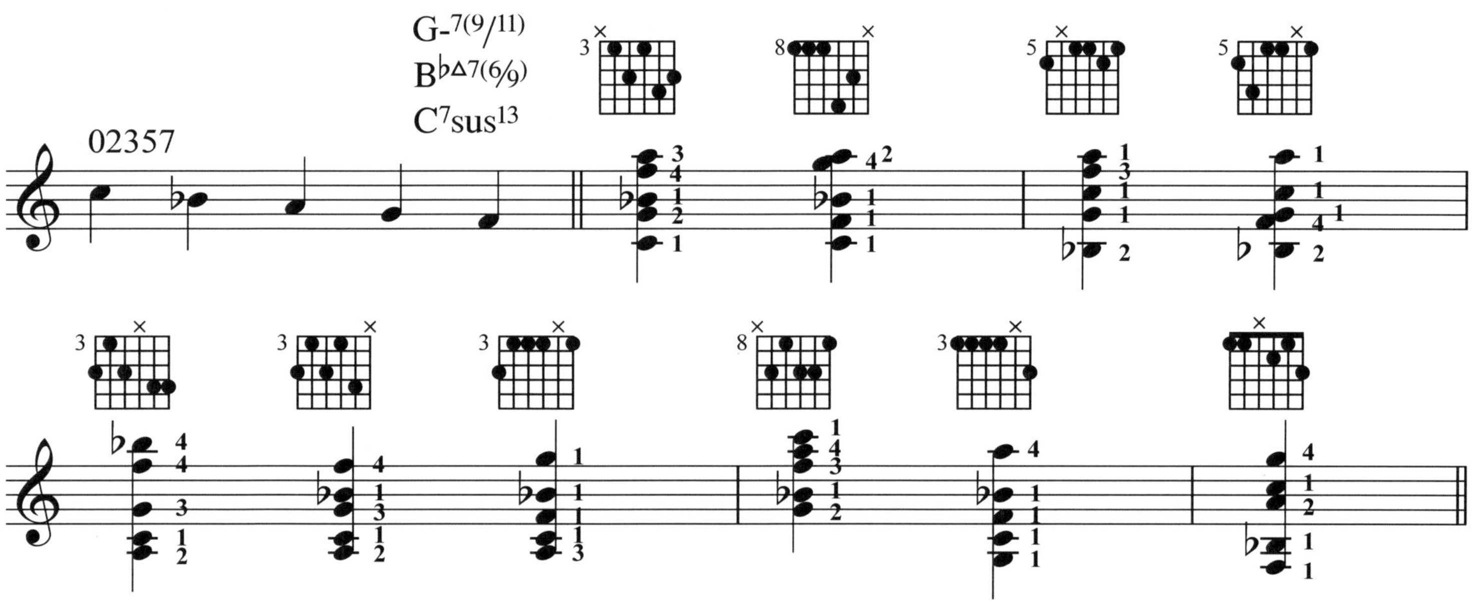
02357
G-7(9/11)
B♭Δ7(6/9)
C7sus13

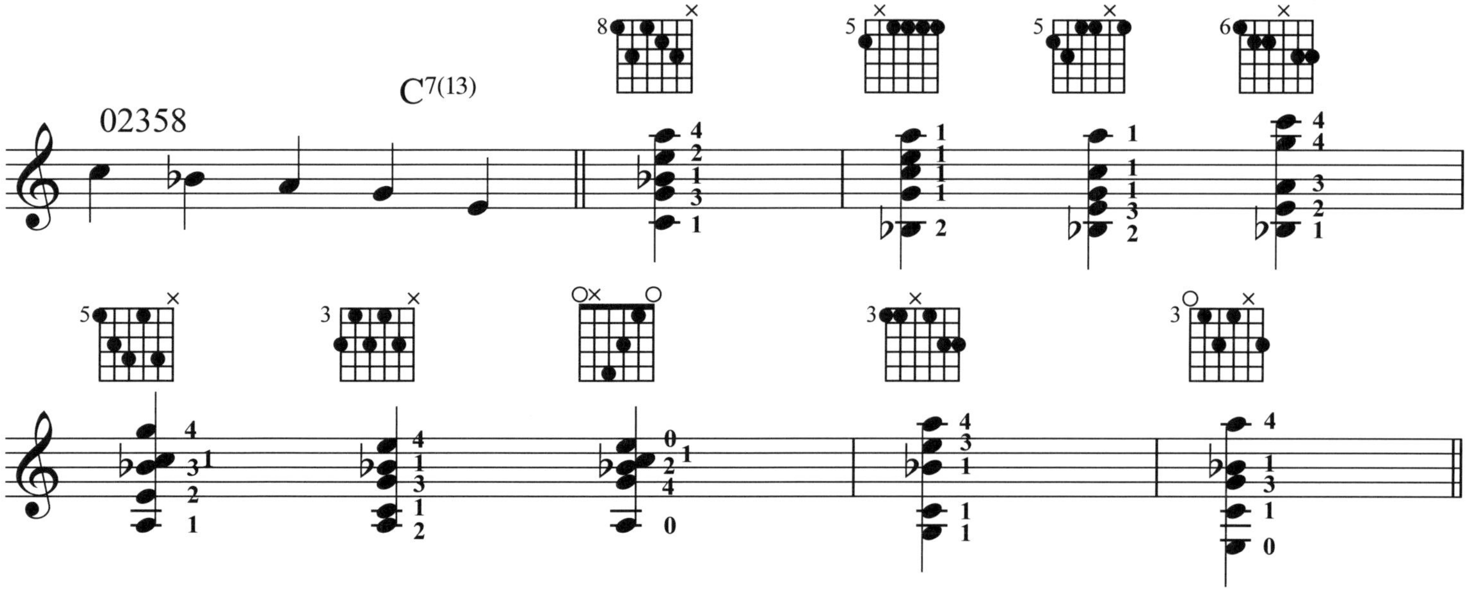
02358
C7(13)

02368
C7(♭5/13)
02458
B♭7(9/♯11/13)
C7(♯5)
02468
A♭7(9/♯5)
G♭7(9/♯11)
Symmetrical (same as 02468, previous section)
02469
A♭7(9)
Symmetrical (same as 02469, previous section)
02479
A♭(6/9)
B♭sus
Symmetrical (same as 02479, previous section)
03458
A♭Δ7(♭9/♯5)
Symmetrical (same as 03458, previous section)

Hexa-Chords

012345
012346
012347
012348
012356
012357
C-/D-Δ7
012358
A♭/D-Δ7
012367
012368
012369
012378
012456
012457
012458
012467
012468
012469
012478
012479
012567
012568
012569
012578
012579
012678
013457
013458

013467
013468
D♭-Δ7(9/11)
A♭7sus(♯5)
013469
013478
E♭7(13/♭9/11)
013479
A7(♭5/♯9)
013568
E♭-7(9/11/13)
G♭Δ7(9/13/♯11)
013569
F/G♭
013578
C-(♯5/♭9/11)
F-7(6/♯5/9)
013579
013679
014568
014579
A7(♯5/♯9)/E
014589
A-/D♭
F-/A
D♭-/F
014679
023457
023458
023468
023469
023568
023579
F7(9/13)
023679
024579
FΔ7(6/9)
D-7(9/11)
02468 10

Hexa-Chords

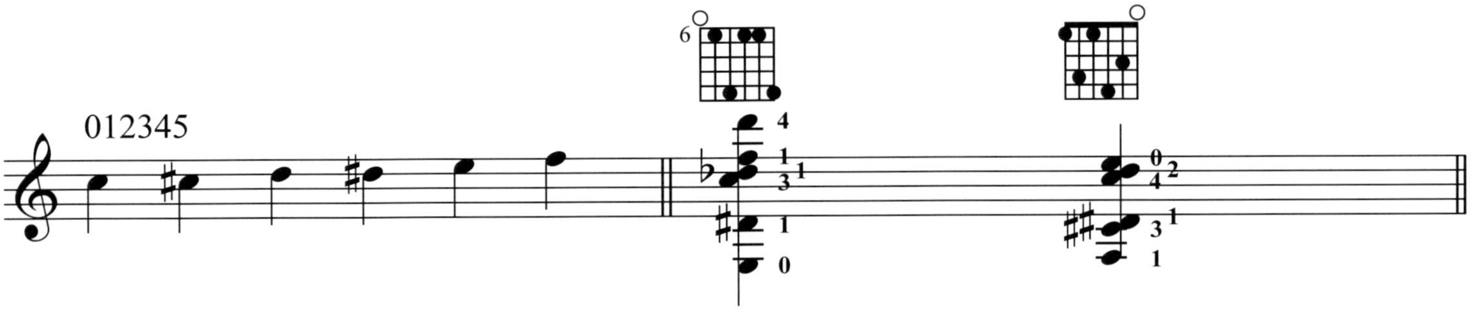

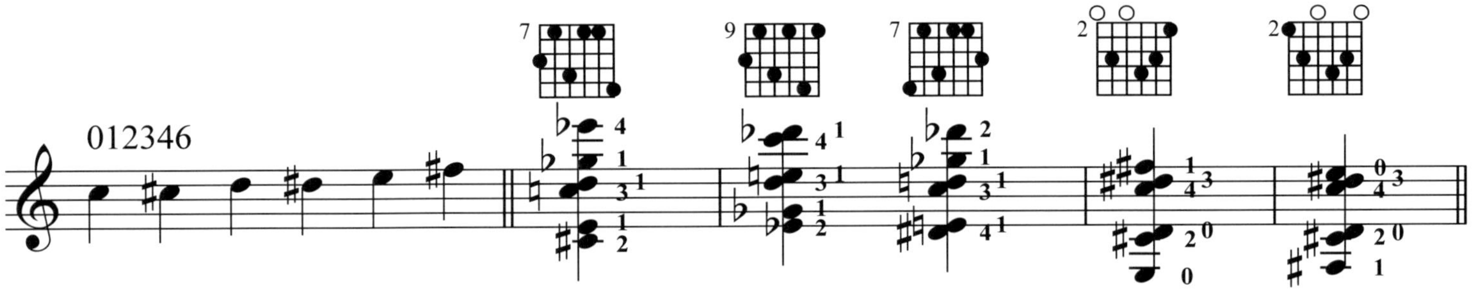

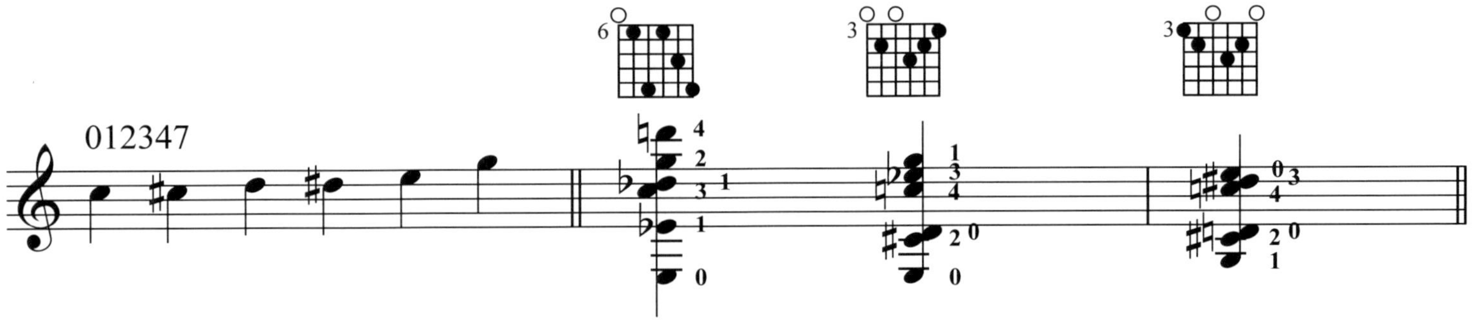

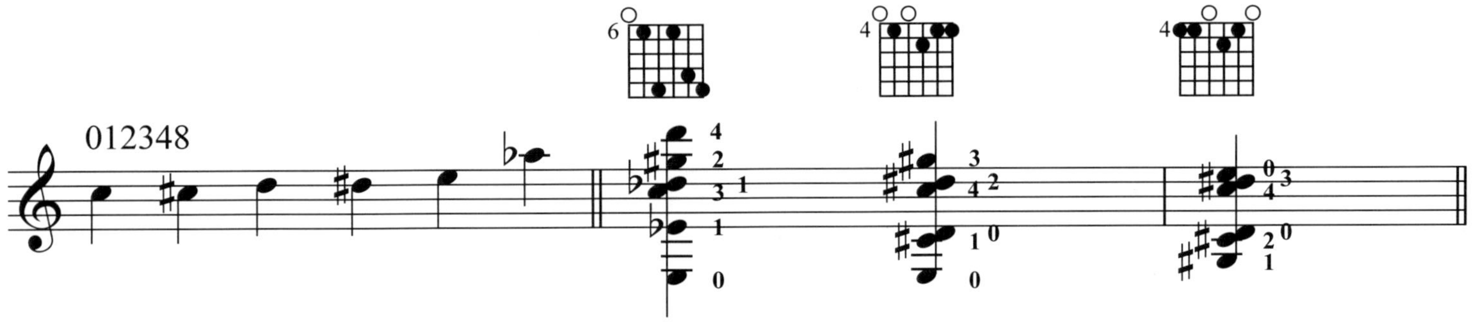

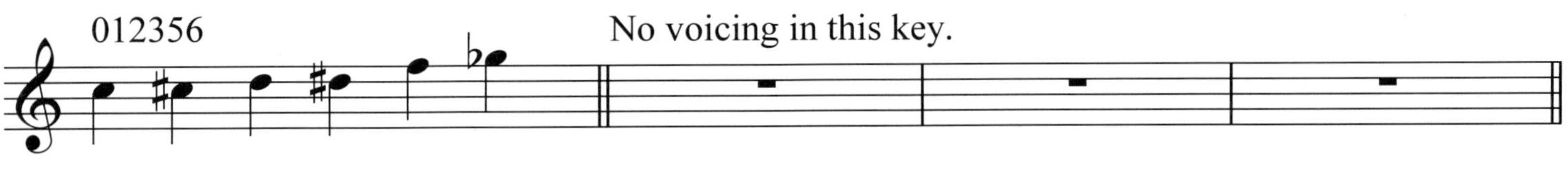

012357
C-/D-Δ7
012358
A♭/D-Δ7
012367
012368
012369
012378

012456
012457
012458
012467
012468
012469

012478
012479
012567
012568
012569
012578

012579
012678
013457
013458

013467
013468
D♭-Δ7(9/11)
A♭7sus(♯5)
013469
013478
E♭7(13/♭9/11)
013479
A7(♭5/♯9)

013568
E♭-7(9/11/13)
G♭Δ7(9/13/♯11)
013569
F/G♭
013578
C-(♯5/♭9/11)
F-7(6/♯5/9)
013579
013679
No voicing in this key.
014568

014579
A7(♯5/♯9)/E
014589
A-/D♭
F-/A
D♭-/F
014679
023457

023458
023468
023469
023568
No voicing in this key.
023579
F7(9/13)

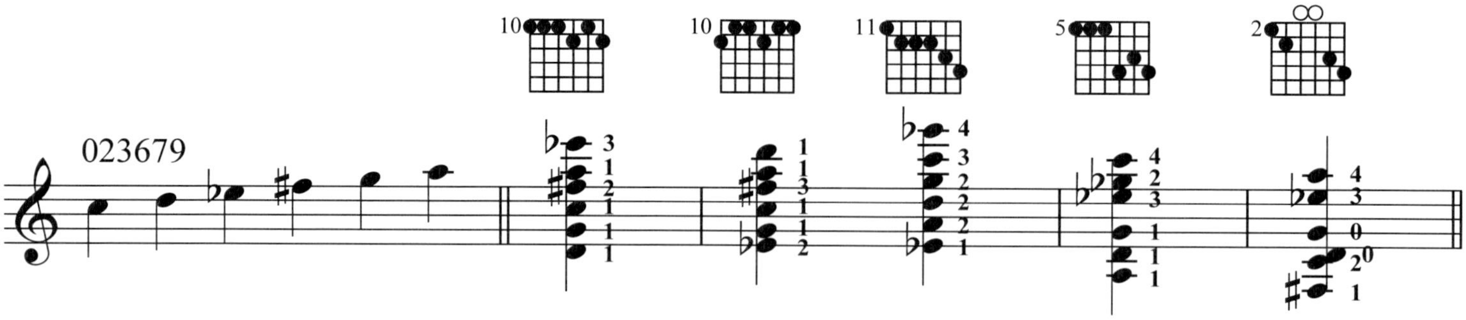
023679

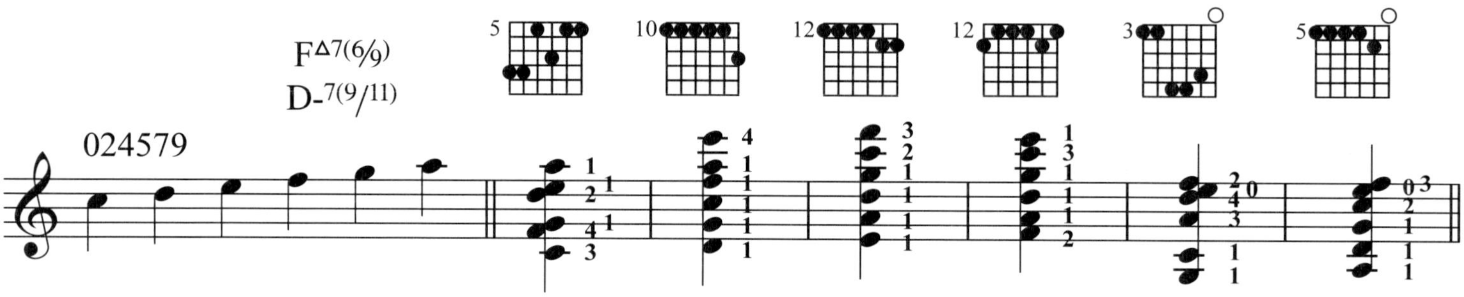
024579
FΔ7(6/9)
D-7(9/11)

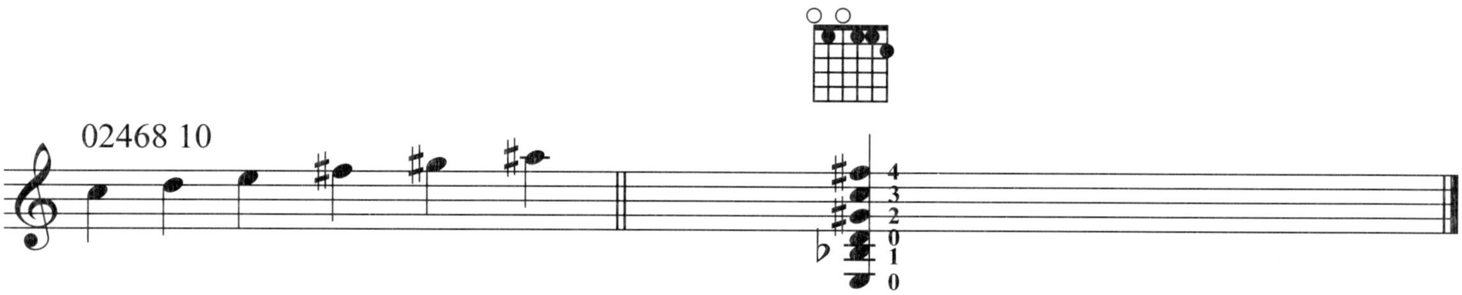
02468 10

Inverted Hexa-Chords

013478
013479
013568
B-7(♯5/♭9)
A-7(13/9)
013569
013578
013579
G7(♯5/9/11)
F7(♭5/9)
013679
014568
014579
014589
014679
023457
023458
023468
023469
023568
023579
G-7(♯5/9/11)
C-7(13/11)
F/E♭
023679
Cø7(13/11)
024579
A♭Δ7(6/9)
C-7(♯5/11)
02468 10

Inverted Hexa-Chords

012357
012358
012367
012368
012369

012378
012456
012457
012458
A♭7(♯9/13/9)
012467
012468

012469
A♭7(♯9/9)
012478
012479
B△7(♭5/13/♭9)
012567
No voicing in this key
012568
012569

012578
012579
012678
Symmetrical (same as 012678, previous section)
013457
013458
013467
(Symmetrical)

A♭7(♯5/♯9/♭9)
A-Δ7(9/13)
013468
013469
A♭7(♯9/♭9)
013478
013479
A-7(13/9)
B-7(♯5/♭9)
013568
013569

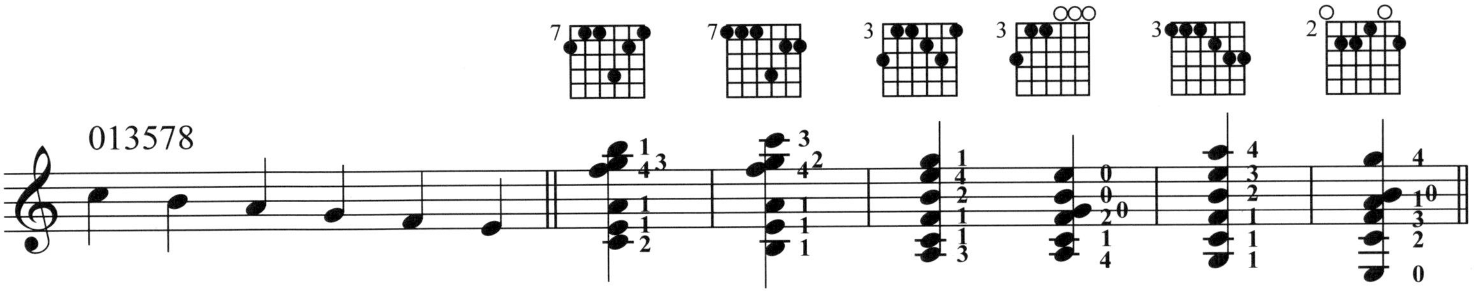
013578

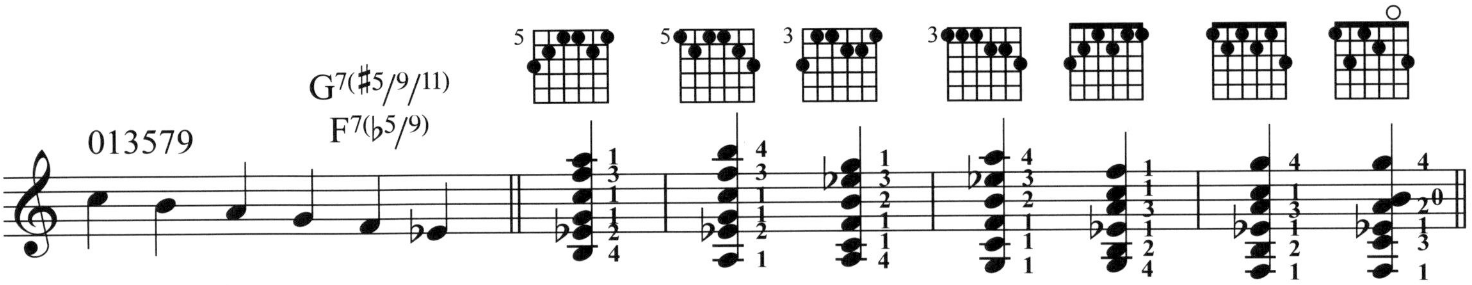
013579
G7(♯5/9/11)
F7(♭5/9)

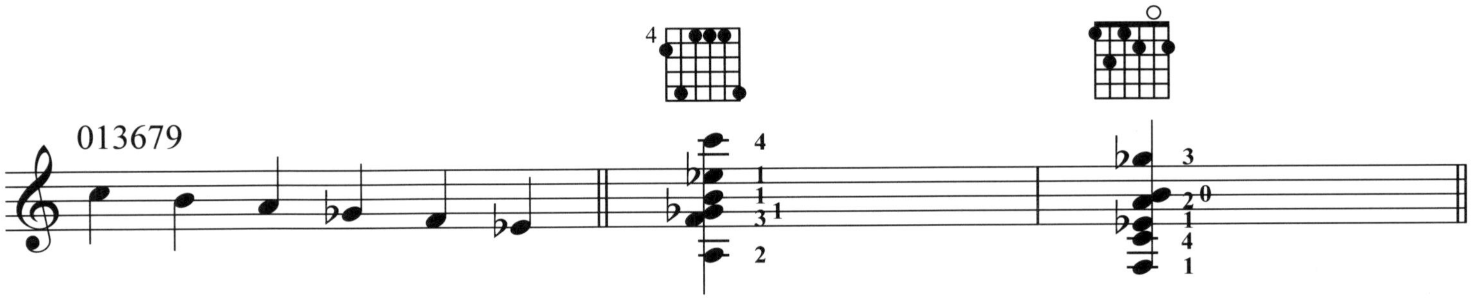
013679

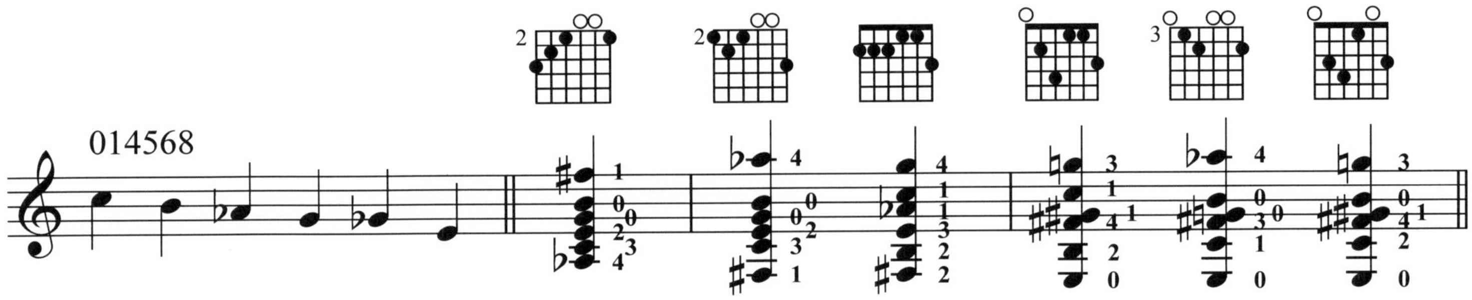
014568

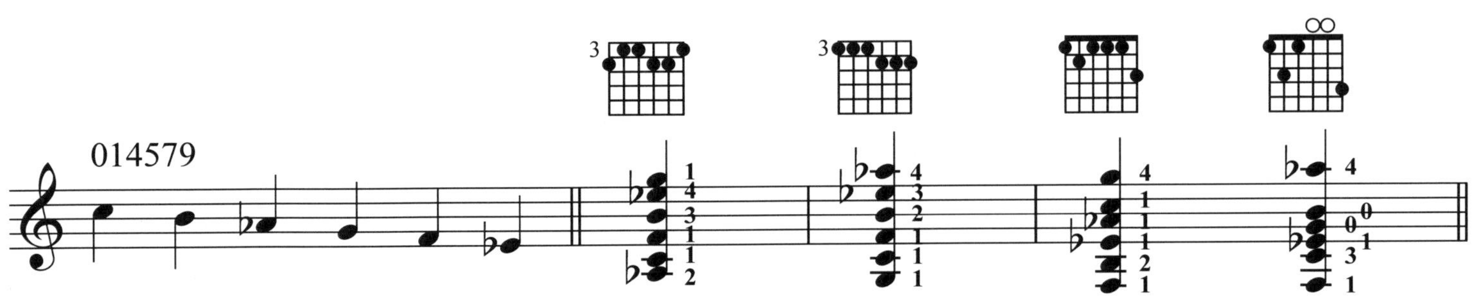
014579

014589
(Symmetrical)
014679
(Symmetrical)
023457
023458
023468
023469

023568
G-7(♯5/9/11)
C-7(13/11)
F/E♭
023579
C∅7(13/11)
023679
(Symmetrical)
A♭Δ7(6/9)
C-7(♯5/11)
024579
(Symmetrical)
02468 10
(Symmetrical)

photo: Esther Blum

I came to New York in 1984 and finished school in '86. During that time, and after, I studied with: Reggie Workman, Henry Martin, Bill Saxton, Chuck Loeb, Pat Martino, Ben Monder, Dave Fiuczynski, Virginia Luque, Mark Delpriora, Rachel Z. and many others.

I've played many styles of music including Jazz, Classical, Blues, Cuban, Brazilian and Avant-Garde music. Actually, I feel like I learned more about music after college than at any other time in my life. To be out there doing it every day, playing with many different people and experiencing their various perspectives on music is irreplaceable. I've always been interested in exploring new chordal ideas and searching for information that would enable me to expand that search. The available books on this subject never satisfied me. This book is a response to a perceived need to show modern chord ideas on the guitar. There are a few good books out there, but there's room for more!

I sincerely hope you enjoy this book, and if you find any new voicings that are not included here, send me an email. In addition, if you have any questions or would like to invite me to teach this material, please feel free to contact me at:

www.bloomworks.com

Enjoy!

1
2
3
4
5
6

1
2
3
4
5
6

1
2
3
4
5
6

1
2
3
4
5
6

1
2
3
4
5
6

MEL BAY PUBLICATIONS, INC. • www.MELBAY.com